6D24X95N

THE NEW APPROACH TO

REAL ESTATE APPRAISING

THE NEW APPROACH TO REAL ESTATE APPRAISING

GENE DILMORE
M.A.I.-S.R.E.A.-A.S.A.

PRENTICE-HALL, INC.
Englewood Cliffs, N.J.

PRENTICE-HALL INTERNATIONAL, INC., *London*
PRENTICE-HALL OF AUSTRALIA, PTY. LTD., *Sydney*
PRENTICE-HALL OF CANADA, LTD., *Toronto*
PRENTICE-HALL OF INDIA PRIVATE LTD., *New Delhi*
PRENTICE-HALL OF JAPAN, INC., *Tokyo*

Library of Congress
Catalog Card Number: 70-141360

"This publication is designed to provide accurate and authoritative information in regard to the subject matter covered. It is sold with the understanding that the publisher is not engaged in rendering legal, accounting or other professional service. If legal advice or other expert assistance is required, the services of a competent professional person should be sought.

...From the Declaration of Principles jointly adopted by a Committee of the American Bar Association and a Committee of Publishers and Associations."

PRINTED IN THE UNITED STATES OF AMERICA
ISBN-0-13-612440-2
B & P

Respectfully dedicated to the memory of

John Rae

—who lived and died questioning.

About the Author

Gene Dilmore, MAI, SREA, ASA, operates a general appraising practice in Birmingham, Alabama, where he specializes in appraising and counseling with respect to investment properties in the southeastern states.

Mr. Dilmore is a member of the American Institute of Real Estate Appraisers, a Senior Real Estate Analyst member of the Society of Real Estate Appraisers, and a Senior member of the American Society of Appraisers. He has served as President of the Birmingham chapter of the Society of Real Estate Appraisers, the Birmingham chapter of the American Society of Appraisers, and the Alabama chapter of the American Institute of Real Estate Appraisers, and is a member of the Editorial Advisory Committee of *The Real Estate Appraiser.*

The author is a former member of the Jefferson County (Birmingham) Board of Equalization, during which time he was in charge of the valuation of Central Business District properties.

Mr. Dilmore has testified extensively in condemnation and corporate share tax cases, and is believed to be the first appraiser to present testimony on commercial property valuations based on multiple regression analyses.

He is also the author of numerous articles on real estate valuation, was a contributor to *Selected Readings In Right of Way,* and lectures frequently on appraisal topics.

A Word from the Author

In the appraisal profession, as elsewhere, variability is the only constant. Both theory and practice are undergoing numerous changes, some superficial, some basic. Grave danger lies in reacting to these changes by rigid adherence to discredited but institutionalized theories and techniques.

It is not necessary to choose between "customary, therefore better," and "different, therefore better." Whether traditional or innovative, appraisal concepts should be judged on their own merits, without regard to preconceived standards.

This book has some negative things to say with regard to some of the traditional appraisal dogmas. Its principal intent, however, is to contribute positively by presenting applications of current thinking to the appraisal process.

The techniques discussed include:

- Discounted cash flow analysis.
- Analysis of proposed modernization, remodeling, or expansion.
- An approach to analysis of market data, including a method of delimitation of the value range, a base property technique of sale or rental comparison, and discussion of market data adjustments.
- Methods used in highest and best use analysis, feasibility studies, market studies, and consultation problems.
- Some practical applications of the Ellwood Process.
- Multiple regression analysis. With the availability of desktop computers and relatively inexpensive time on larger computers, regression analysis is now practicable for even the small office. Although the process is usually computerized, in my opinion the appraiser should not use the results without knowing what steps the computer is performing, as his interpretation of the analysis could otherwise be incorrect. For this reason, three chapters are devoted to a step-by-step introduction to this process, which I think will become one of the standard tools of the appraiser in the near future.

The debt of anyone writing on appraising, to Frederick Babcock, Richard U. Ratcliff, L. W. Ellwood, Irving Fisher, and K. Lee Hyder, almost goes without saying. My thanks go to Wayne D. Hagood, for an entirely constructive review of the manuscript, to the Society of Real Estate Appraisers for permission to use in Chapters X and XI material originally published in *The Real Estate Appraiser,* and to the Appraisal Institute of Canada for permission to use in Chapters VI and VIII material originally published in *The Appraisal Institute Magazine.*

Gene Dilmore

Contents

I

New Thinking in the
Valuation Process: Interrelation of
Appraisal Function,
Objective, and Technique

$\mathbf{T}$he real estate market is basically a rational institution, and its analysis is a science.

Although there is no exactly correct answer to any real estate valuation problem, there is, under any given set of conditions, one solution with a higher degree of probability than any other. This implies that real estate valuation is not primarily a matter of "judgment and experience," but is primarily a matter of logical analysis of a methodically drawn sample of the real estate market. It implies that subjectively generated data can be objectively analyzed. And it implies that the appraisal process consists in the orderly and systematic definition and solution of sometimes complex but always solvable problems.

Past and Present:

In the 1930's, two figures stood at the forefront of appraisal thinking: Frederick M. Babcock, whose "Valuation of Real Estate" still remains the basic treatise on real estate valuation principles, and Richard U. Ratcliff, who urged adaptation of sound economic theory and practice to the appraisal field.

In considering the most advanced current thinking in real estate valuation theory, it is necessary, ironically enough, to turn again to Babcock and Ratcliff. The two major points presently being urged by Babcock are:

1. That his original discussion of three valuation approaches, which were applied to three separate types of property, has been completely distorted in the so-called "Three Approach" doctrine, which erroneously states that the value of a specific property is indicated by three separate approaches to the value, after which the three approaches are "correlated" into a final value estimate.
2. That the major variable in each appraisal is the purpose or function of the appraisal.

The major propositions currently being expounded by Ratcliff include:

1. That the most usual purpose of an appraisal is to estimate the most probable selling price. While this must sound to a non-appraiser like an obvious truism, this thinking is still not given credence in the vast majority of appraisals.
2. That each valuation is a prediction made under definable terms of uncertainty.
3. That each appraisal is needed in order that a specific decision be made or a specific action be taken, and should be approached accordingly.

Future:

In the immediate future the appraisal practitioner will need to acquaint himself with five major fields of "new thinking":

1. He must, somehow, achieve the maturity and the courage to break out of the "three-approach bind," and discard the demonstrably false methodology it requires.
2. The utility of inferential statistics and probability analysis has been apparent since the 1920's, when regression analyses were employed in valuation of farm properties. During the appraisal profession's recent equivalent of the Dark Ages, however, these useful tools have been generally ignored by the profession.
3. Modern business methods of mathematical analysis, including model building and simulation, capital budgeting, and investment analysis, are applicable in many valuation problems. These mathematical tools, already in use in many large businesses, particularly as to location analysis and marketing strategy, will soon be required equipment for the proficient real estate appraiser.
4. Computer usage in the valuation field may be considered in three distinct processes:

    A. Data storage and retrieval (example—sale data, classified in any manner desired).

    B. Analyses of large quantities of data (example—correlation and regression analysis).

    C. Fast handling of repetitive calculation (example—investment analyses, feasibility studies of numerous alternative project configurations).

5. Process analyses, including the several methods of plotting a flow of work, such as PERT (Program Evaluation and Review Technique), and CPM (Critical Path Method), are highly adaptable, particularly to large appraisal projects, and can be used even on smaller projects with beneficial results as to the proper alignment of activity sequences for the most efficient completion of the project.

New Types of Reports:

As the problems of businessmen and governmental agencies with respect to real estate decisions become more complex, new types of reports are being required, some of which are considerably removed from the original conception of an appraisal report and derivation of a single value figure as the end product of the appraiser's analysis. Among these are:

1. Highest and Best Use Studies
2. Feasibility Studies
3. Land Utilization and Marketability Studies
4. Market Surveys
5. Location Analyses
6. Discounted Cash Flow Analyses of Proposed Investments.

"Real Estate" or "Urban Economics"?

More and more, the product with which the appraiser must cope is not simply "real estate," but a conglomerate of several disciplines, so that he is increasingly participating in an interdisciplinary profession.

The many interlocking factors involved in value of land and/or improvements, particularly as to urban properties, mean that the appraiser will find himself increasingly unusable unless he masters the elements of the related disciplines, including economics, sociology, psychology, demography, econometrics, planning, transportation, communications, urban political forces, merchandising methods and trends, and other related fields. Many factors other than land costs and building costs interlock and react upon the product which the appraiser has heretofore considered to comprise merely "real estate."

The "generalist" nature of his work requires more than a passing acquaintance with these various urban studies, which might possibly be grouped together under the heading of "urbanistics," or "urbanology," both of which terms comprise more sub-factors than either "real estate" or "urban economics," and do not imply a political stance as does "urbanism."

New Concepts:

Among the many emerging concepts with which the appraiser must cope, the following typify the revisions which must be made to the presently institutionalized dogmas:

1. There can be more than one highest and best use for a property.
2. Valuation of an improved property cannot properly consider the land "as if vacant."
3. The cost of a property consists, not of the cost of land plus cost of building only, but includes the further item of the entrepreneurial factor.
4. The value of land can and does depreciate.
5. All appraisals are erroneous, some merely being less erroneous than others. The value estimate is not a denotative fact, but the expression of a probability with a given range of error, which can be expressed with a reasonable degree of precision.
6. The appraiser does help to make the market, and he does create value. His appraisals precipitate decisions which constitute the basis of the market and of its values.
7. A number of items of practice and technique, such as plottage and corner influence, are grossly abused by misconception of the types of properties to which they are applicable.
8. Stabilized income projections cannot properly reflect the present value of an investment.
9. The "breakdown" method and the "capitalized rent loss" method of depreciation estimation, while impressive to some uninformed clients, are mathematically absurd, and the appraiser abrades his integrity through their use.

Purpose and Function Shape the Process:

The purpose and the function of an appraisal are key elements in the adoption of the particular process of valuation. The process of the appraisal should be fitted to:

1. The property characteristics.
2. The specific problem of a specific client, which is not necessarily an estimate of market value as classically defined.
3. Terms of the specific transaction or decision contemplated.

The Three Approaches:

The fallacious concept of a market value estimate supported by the three legs of a tripod consisting of the Market Data Approach, the Income Approach, and the Cost Approach, must be disposed of before appraisers can address themselves to the estimation of the market value of real property.

In each valuation, the appraiser normally reaches a value conclusion by one process or "approach," as he knows that, in the vast majority of cases, one only is basically applicable to each property type. Once he has arrived at his decision as to an approximate value, the contrivance of two more "approaches," purporting to substantiate his value estimate, is dishonest and unworthy of a man aspiring to a learned profession.

The basic logic of the "three approaches" was stated most succinctly in the old saw: "I've said it once; I've said it twice; when I say it three times it will be true."

The Present Work as an Interim Study:

Appraisers should have approximately the same type and amount of education (as distinguished from two weeks' trade training courses) as planners and economists, since the basic ingredients of their profession are approximately the same.

The present work, therefore, may be considered as an interim study only, designed for the specific purpose of filling a need by the professional practitioner who cannot go back and acquire the minimum of six years education which the practice of his profession warrants, but who can familiarize himself with current trends, and make selective further study of particular facets of current appraisal thinking which are most applicable to his own practice.

II

The Appraisal Process

Whether it be a single family residence or a large industrial plant, each appraisal or consultation assignment is a problem capable of a rational and systematic solution. Activities in the real estate market are, on the whole, of an orderly nature, and may be successfully analyzed by an orderly process. The process of evaluation appears to me to proceed in the following steps:

1. Purpose.

What is the purpose of the assignment? What decision is being made? Does the client need a selling price, buy or not buy advice, a rent survey, a feasibility study, a management survey, a highest and best use study? The type of answer needed determines the data program and the methodology required.

2. Function.

How is the appraisal to be used—for lending, borrowing, to set a lease, to make an offer, for condemnation, etc.? The function determines what sort of information is supplied in the report, and in what format the answers are presented.

25

3. The Client.

The appraisal should be tailored to the specific client. What are his investment objectives, his financial position, tax position, specific needs, degree and area of expertise? How does he weight probability of loss against probability of gain? Is certainty of income more important to him than chance of enhancement? An analysis of an investment property for a specific client is virtually meaningless unless reduced to an after-tax equity-yield basis.

4. Context.

The property is established within its geographical and economic context. The appraiser narrows his focus from the region to the community, to the neighborhood, to the site, searching at each level for clues to future trends. Supply and demand are analyzed for indications as to the property's marketability.

5. Capital Structure.

A realistic appraisal cannot be made unless the appraiser knows the financing available.

6. Property Rights.

Each parcel of real property comprises certain specified rights to perform or not perform certain acts with respect to the property. These rights must be precisely identified.

7. Property Type.

What basic type of property is being appraised—amenity property, income property, or special purpose property? What alternatives are available—purchase, lease, or build? What data are available?

8. Processing the Data.

A. If an amenity property is being appraised, it should be valued by sale comparisons. If sufficient data are available, multiple regression analysis is often a logical and proper process of valuation. If a lesser but still substantial number of sales are available, delimitation of the value range is the most desirable process. If data are fairly scarce, then either individual adjustments or overall comparative ratings may be used. Cost computations and income imputations are irrelevant to the problem.

B. If an income property is being appraised, direct sale comparison using gross or net return as the pricing unit is generally the primary basis of valuation. Sale comparison by regression analysis is also often feasible. Gross and net income furnish the most useful dependent variables.

For counseling or investment analysis, replacement cost should be calculated for proposed improvements, not for valuation purposes, but so that the return on the given investment can be calculated. In investment analysis, care should be taken that all five possible sources of income are accounted for, and year by year income fluctuations are projected when feasible. A discounted cash flow analysis should be made, on a net after-tax equity-yield basis.

✗ C. If a special purpose property is being appraised, it should be valued on the basis of substituting real alternatives.

(1) Build—What would it cost to construct a building which will fill the subject property's function—(not necessarily physically similar), and what would an available alternative site cost—not the hypothetical cost of the subject site, but the cost of a real alternative property.

(2) Buy—A substitute property which, again, does not necessarily physically resemble the subject property, but can serve its function.

(3) Rent—A rental substitute should be considered if one is available and is a likely alternative. This does not mean to consider what the subject would rent for if it were rented, but at what rental an actual likely alternative is available.

Finally, when the foregoing eight steps have been taken, write a report in which you simply tell the client what the problem was, how you went about solving it, and what the solution was. The essential elements of the report are property description, data program, methodology, and conclusions.

Do not strain the intelligent client's credulity by pretending to correlate three entirely disquiparant valuation processes: You have made one appraisal, not three, and professional integrity demands that you—simply and honestly—present that appraisal in such a manner as competently to guide the client's decision-making policy.

III

Land Use and Forces of
City Growth: Components of
Real Estate Value

Determine what your selling before determination of whom your going to sell it to

I n order to grasp an idea of the multitude of economic forces acting upon a specific property, the appraiser must be able to place the property within its regional context.

1. The first step in this process is to test the boundaries of the region. In some cases these boundaries will be sharply defined, either by natural or man-made barriers while in other cases, the limit of regional development must be drawn with a certain amount of arbitrariness.

2. The existing and proposed street and highway patterns and transportation facilities must be studied with respect to their effect on the property.

3. Directions of growth should be identified, and the causes for the development should be analyzed. It should be established whether and to what extent subject property is affected by these directions of growth.

4. Rather than a mere collection of land and buildings, the region is more properly conceived of as a synergic complex of activities, with the use of land and buildings not causing but being *caused by* these activities: The land and buildings are subordinate to, and serve to house, these functions and activities.

31

5. Statistical data for the region should be analyzed. The most relevant data include employment, population, income, sale data, land uses and vacancies. The basic generative force creating value in any region is employment opportunity.

All information, both that derived from published materials and that derived from on-site inspection, must be analyzed as to its specific effect on subject property to:

a. Establish rate of growth or decline.
b. Identify causes of growth or decline.
c. Compare with other trends (state and national).
d. Project stability of region.
e. Deduce from these factors a prediction of the *most probable* future of subject.

Regional trends must be related directly to subject, as these trends indicate the direction and velocity of the market, which is only reflected as of certain *past* dates by market transactions.

Kinds of Cities:

Narrowing the focus of your analysis from the region to the city, you note that the city will be predominantly oriented toward one or more of the following basic classifications:

1. Commercial
2. Industrial
3. Extractive
4. Political
5. Social Centers, Health Resorts, and Retirement Communities
6. Financial
7. Educational
8. Agricultural

Although such classifications are descriptive rather than predictive, these bear upon your analysis of trends, and it is important that you be aware of the extend of diversification, and of the expectable economic strength particularly of the primary, or export, functions of the subject city.

How Cities Grow:

Cities have grown generally from the point of a change in form of transportation, or an intersection of transportation lines.

Several theories of city growth have been advanced, none of which is purported to be a replication of the inconceivably numerous forces of growth; but they are designed as idealized arrangements of the underlying force of growth.

1. Richard Hurd[1] in 1903, differentiated between centrality and axiality of growth, and pointed out the interaction of the two forces, with growth following the line of least resistance along transportation routes, being followed by expansion of the central growth area.
2. In 1925, Burgess[2] propounded the concentric ring theory, which envisioned growth expanding directly outward from the center of the city, with this idealized picture of the city being modified to the extent that growth spread outward principally along the main routes of transportation, and along physical barriers such as a water front.
3. Hoyt's[3] sector theory, proposed in 1939, pictured city growth for the various land uses as spreading out in generally pie shaped wedges from the center of the city.
4. Though earlier in time than Hoyt's theory, the concept of multiple nuclei by R. D. McKenzie,[4] in 1933, is, in effect, a refinement of the sector theory.

From observation the appraiser can see that most or all of the concepts are to some extent involved in the outward growth of each city. The most accessible transportation routes and the location of the highest grade residential areas are magnetic factors in each city, of which the appraiser must be keenly aware when estimating trends or patterns of future growth of the city.

Urban Economic Background:

The economic background of the city may be analyzed to whatever degree of elaboration is desired, with some such studies costing several hundred thousand dollars. Since the real estate appraiser or consultant is not generally compensated for a year long study, every shortcut available must be utilized in analyzing the economic base of the subject city.

One such rough estimate approach to the analysis of the economic background of a community is by use of FHA Form Number 2096, devised in 1936 by Homer Hoyt.[5] This Economic Background Rating Form briefly summarized indicated economic trends of the community.

[1] Richard M. Hurd, "Principles of City Land Values," New York, The Record and Guide, 1903, Copyright 1924, R. M. Hurd.

[2] Earnest W. Burgess, "The Growth of the City" in R. E. Park, et al, editors The City, Chicago, University of Chicago Press, 1925.

[3] Homer Hoyt, "The Structure and Growth of Residential Neighborhoods in American Cities," Washington, D. C., F. H. A., 1939. U. S. Government Printing Office, 1939.

[4] R. D. McKenzie, The Metropolitan Community, New York, McGraw-Hill Book Company, Inc., 1933.

[5] Federal Housing Administration, "Underwriting Manual," Paragraph 1504-1510, Rev. 1958.

In Hoyt's process, economic activities are divided into three categories:

1. Industry
2. Specialty
3. Trade

The classification of specialty employment includes tourism and retirement, education, and political activity.

The industry and specialty categories are multiplied by two, on the assumption that one service worker is required for each industry or specialty employee in basic or export activities. The figure for trade, therefore, is arrived at by subtraction of the doubled percentage for the other two categories from 100, which leaves the percentage in trade. The percentage of employment in each of these three groups determines the weight given to sub-headings under each of these categories.

The industry category is analyzed as to predicted employment trends, diversification, and cyclical fluctuations, with variances in these factors being weighted by the category weight applicable. The specialty and the trade category are rated only on predicted employment trend and cyclical fluctuations, each being given one of five classification weights.

The sum of these applicable category ratings is then weighted by a figure for "scope of the market," reflecting the degree of marketability, and resulting in an overall rating of the community's economic background. Use of this form was originally contemplated for housing markets, but it can be applied to the economic background study of a community which is necessary for the appraisal of any type of property.

A further suggested modification of this form is an attempt to establish a more exact ratio of services to industry and service to specialty employment, for, as Hoyt himself soon discovered, his original assumption of a one-to-one ratio was not precisely correct, but the ratio ran roughly from one-to-one, to two-to-one in various cities.

Objections to Economic Base Theory:

Hoyt's approach to this problem was the major contribution to Economic Base theory. He assumed, originally, that all industrial activity was basic (variously called primary or export activity). It is apparent, however, that this is not true of all cities.

Several other objections to the theory arise:

1. The larger the area under study, the less the validity.
2. It assumes that a balance of payments situation is definitionally "good" when exports exceed imports. If this were correct, only approximately 50% of the cities in the country would be growing, and the other 50% would be declining. This proposition, of course, could not stand under empirical testing.
3. The "basic" activities do not necessarily support the city's growth.
4. Indirect basic employment is not identified.

5. It does not identify the industries which are most vulnerable to outside forces.

6. It does not identify payments for other goods or services.

7. The method is weakened by linkages of industrial and commercial activities, and cannot account for feedback between basic and non-basic activities.

Revisions of Economic Base:

Hoyt has revised[6] this process to facilitate its use in forecasting population, as follows:

1. Calculate employment in each basic industry.
2. Estimate ratio of basic to service employment.
3. Estimate ratio of total population to employment.
4. Estimate future trend of basic employment.
5. Derive future total employment, and population from employment projection.

Steps 2 and 3 are often omitted, with use of population to employment ratio of 7 to 1.

Localizational Quotient:

An alternative method[7] of estimating basic and non-basic (export and import) items is as follows:

1. Extract ratio of employment or industry classification to population of study area.
2. Make same calculation for U.S. total (available in census data).
3. Assume average of local employment above national average is the export, or basic item, as it is the amount more than that needed (on the average) to support the community only. Therefore Item #1 minus Item #2 = basic employment.

These relations are sometimes expressed as a localization quotient,[8] in the form:

$$\frac{\text{Local Employment in Industry A}}{\text{Total Employment in City}} \Big/ \frac{\text{National Employment in Industry A}}{\text{Total National Employment}}$$

A quotient higher than one indicates that the particular local industry is a basic or

---

[6] Homer Hoyt and A. M. Weiner, *Principles of Real Estate* (4th edition; New York: Ronald Press, 1960).

[7] New York Regional Plan Association, "The Economic Status of the New York Metropolitan Region," New York, 1944.

[8] Harold M. Mayer, "Urban Nodality and the Economic Base," *Journal of the American Institute of Planners,* Summer, 1954.

"export" industry, while a quotient lower than one indicates that the city imports the goods or services of this industry.

The purpose of arriving at the ratio of basic or primary employment to total population is, fundamentally, to project population in order to estimate and interpret trends, and to predict total effect on the local economy from establishment or expansion of a specific industry.

The principal statistical trends of interest to the appraiser are employment, population, family or per capita income, housing, and retail sales. Comparisons should be made on 3 levels: local, state, and national. In this way, trends peculiar to the community may be pinpointed.

Analysis of a city's economy may, of course, be considerably refined, for planning uses, with other techniques, especially input-output analyses, being much more descriptive of a community's economy. This method, however, is too time-consuming for the appraiser's purposes which, at this point, are to establish contextual trends and to analyze the fairly short term prospects of a specific property within its established milieu.

Land Use Arrangements:

A land use study of the city is a vital part of your analysis. If a recent economic study, to which you have access, has been made much time can be saved; otherwise you must make the best estimate you can in the allotted time as to the portions of land used for different purposes.

The starting point for this study may be the city's zoning map which will show the amount and location of land zoned for residential, residential income, commercial and industrial use, with uses sometime being broken down into subsections of the foregoing. You can then inspect the variously zoned sections, making your own rough estimate as to the extent of use in each zoning area.

In seeking to establish the directions and extent of growth of particular land uses, bear in mind that the zoning does not automatically result in such use: The land and buildings merely serve to house a complex of functions or activities, and it is the effective demand for these activities, as modified by local physical, social, political, and economic factors, which will determine the pattern of land usage.

Economic Components of Real Estate Value:

The economic factors which go to make up the value of the property are, of course, innumerable. They may, however, be reduced to a somewhat more manageable number of categories by selecting value determinants which reflect large subgroups of economic factors.

Obviously, the first requisite for the existence of a real estate value is the existence of a person who desired that parcel of real estate. We may say, then, that the basic component of value is people, or population. The mere existence of a person, however, with a desire for the property, does not ensure the value for that property, as demand is not effective unless the person possesses money or equivalent with which to purchase the property.

To obtain this money several methods are available, but all of these avenues come down in the end to a necessity at some point for the income to have been earned by employment. Thus we arrive at the conclusion that the most vital statistic of all with respect to real estate is *employment* and that the most important variant with respect to employment is the amount of income derived therefrom.

It is assumed that the practicing appraiser is familiar with the available census data relevant to his working territory. Many, however, are unaware of the numerous and important conclusions implied by these "dry statistics."

For instance, analysis of the age group of the population, along with family formation figures and family income figures, may indicate quite clearly that for a given period, and in a given place, a particular client could hardly fail to succeed in the construction and marketing of a large, predominantly one-bedroom apartment project.

An analysis of the same date may likewise indicate that the odds are greatly against a proposed subdivision of two and three bedroom residences. It is part of your job, then, to analyze these statistical data as carefully as you would individual sale data, and to relate the inferred conclusions to the property under consideration.

The Central Business District:

After reaching 100% development, central business districts have a tendency to decline, partly because of estate and absentee owenership, income and property tax considerations, and partly as a consequence of inaccessibility by automobile.

Many efforts at revitalization of the CBD have been made. Methods of approaching the downtown problem include:

1. Redesign of the central area.
2. Shopping malls for pedestrian traffic only.
3. Modernization of the zoning requirements.
4. Grouping of linked uses.
5. Fostering of improvements with shared open spaces (applicable to both commercial and residential properties).
6. Re-development removing the 100% site to a more currently logical and accessible location.
7. Provision of central and/or peripheral parking for optimum service to both autos and pedestrians.

Basic steps conducive to recovery of the downtown area include "metro" government, tax equalization with provision for enforcement, efficient mass transit, and re-establishment of close-in residential areas.

When working in an unfamiliar city, one of the first things the appraiser needs to do is to inspect the master plan of the city, and learn what urban renewal projects may be contemplated. If this is not done, an appraisal may be completed based on entirely false assumptions as to the 100% district and its direction of growth.

Since valuation is a discounting of anticipated future benefits to their present worth, factual data are useful only to the extent that they aid us in projecting trends. And the appraiser must constantly remind himself that all the data gathered and ordered for analysis relate to past occurrences, and are useful only as guideposts for predicting—with whatever degree of uncertainty and imprecision— future occurrences.

Delineating
Neighborhoods and Trading
Areas; Community and Neighborhood
Trend Analysis; Turning Economic
Background Data into
Value Factors

$\mathbf{B}$asically, a neighborhood may be defined as an area of common economic characteristics. Its other characteristics, whether social, political, or topographical, are of importance to the appraiser only insofar as they are reflected in the economic factors affecting the given area.

After consideration of the economic background of the entire subject community, the neighborhood boundaries are delineated. This generally serves two purposes:

1. Sharpening the identification of subject property in its economic context.
2. Bounding the area in which comparable market data are sought, or in which similar factors impinge on subject.

In many cases, one or more of the boundary lines of the neighborhood consists of physical barriers: a highway, railway, river, steep embankment, etc. In some areas the neighborhood characteristics will shade off almost imperceptibly so that no exact point may be said to be precisely on the boundary of the neighborhood. It can, however, be approximated sufficiently for appraisal purposes.

You will find quite often that the neighborhood will coincide fairly consistently with the Census Tract in which the property lies, or within several clearly defined Census Tracts.

Selecting Relevant Neighborhood Characteristics:

For a retail store property, the pertinent area is the trading area, from which a reasonably identifiable share of sales may be drawn.

In a residential neighborhood, an appraiser should so delineate the area that it includes the economic, social, and housing characteristics in common with subject property. Relevant factors include:

1. Employment
2. Family incomes
3. Size of family
4. Median ages
5. Predominant age groups
6. Size and range of value of houses
7. Proportion of owner- and renter-occupied houses

Trading Area:

Boundaries of a trading area, whether of a free-standing store or of a shopping center, can be delineated on the basis of percentage of sales or dollar amount of sales generated.

For example, the primary trading area may be considered to be that in which 70% of subject properties trade will be generated, the secondary trading area accounting for the next 20%, and the tertiary or fringe trading area accounting for the remaining 10%.

The primary trading area may also be considered that within which 75¢ or more per capita sales per week are generated; the secondary trading area including the sales from 25¢ to 75¢ per capita; the fringe area being that generating less than 25¢ per capita per week.

Gravity Model:

The trading area problem is different for each of the two cases of an existing shopping center, in which the drawing power may be measured by observation, and for a proposed shopping center for which comparable centers must be observed and analyzed. In both cases, you may want to check your results against a gravity model, such as Reilly's Principle of Retail Gravitation. Reilly's Principle may be stated as follows:

$$D_{ab} = \frac{d}{1 + \sqrt{P_b/P_a}}$$

where

d = distance in miles on major road between two towns, Towns A and B

P_a = population of Town A

P_b = population of Town B

D_{ab} = limit of Town A trading area measured in miles along the road toward Town B

This equation was first enunciated to measure the breaking point in the drawing power of one town as compared to its competitive town. It has, however, been adapted and used for smaller areas, such as free-standing stores and shopping centers.

As an example of Reilly's Principle, considering A and B to be either towns or shopping centers, and considering D to be either miles or driving minutes, we assume the following:

Population of A = 40,000
Population of B = 10,000
Distance between the two shopping areas is
    30 miles

Then,

$$D_{ab} = \frac{30}{1 + \sqrt{10,000/40,000}}$$

$$= \frac{30}{1 + \sqrt{.25}} = \frac{30}{1.5} = 20 \text{ miles}$$

Therefore, the breaking point of the trading area from the larger shopping area is 20 miles.

This formula at present is often modified by substituting the square feet of sales area for population, and substituting distance in driving time rather than in road miles. Any such formula, of course, should be checked empirically, as a trading area is not a permanent geographical datum, but is a current reflection of individual reactions and decisions.

Comparison Approach:

Empirical, or "on the ground" delineation of the trading area begins with surveys of comparable stores. This may start with interview of purchasers, or by checking automobile tag numbers, after which the addresses of the owners are found in the license office reocrds. Location of each customer in the sampling is then spotted on a customer's spotting map.

The totals of these purchaser surveys may then be grouped within concentric circles from the store or shopping center, either by distance, at half-mile intervals, or by driving time, at five, ten, and fifteen minute driving time intervals. Effective buying power in these areas may be established by personal interviews, or estimated from figures given by the Annual Survey of Buying Power of *Sales Management* Magazine.

When the trading area of a proposed store or center is being estimated, the most practicable approach is by comparison of the subject property location with others in the area for which existing trading areas have been established.

Population:

There are nine chances out of ten that you will be working in a year for which census data on the population in these established areas are not available. The latest census data may be updated by one of two major methods:

1. By checking birth and death rates and in and out migrations.
2. By tabulation of dwelling unit construction, then ascertainment of ratios of population increase to the dwelling units of a prior period, followed by application of this ratio to the new dwelling units built since the last census. This figure will encompass births, deaths, and in and out migrations, all of which are reflected in the one net figure.

For a projection of future expectable population in the trading areas, the percentage expected in either national or state population projections may be applied to the subject area, with such adjustments as are indicated by the non-comparability of subject with either national or state trends. (Updated figures for state and national populations are available from the Census Bureau.) A five-year period is approximately the maximum for which a population projection would have any validity.

Income:

A family income map also should be prepared. When data for the census tracts are not available, the median income for the Standard Metropolitan Statistical Area for the urban area may be used as a base, with the appraiser inspecting the area and rating each neighborhood zone as above or below the median, according to appearance of the neighborhood and to the housing conditions.

Maps:

In delineating a trading area, five types of maps are desirable.

1. Land use map for the immediate area
2. Population map
3. Competition map
4. Customer distribution map
5. Income map

Statistics:

Census data, including census tract information and city block data, are published every ten years. Census data may be updated as described above for population information, and also by comparison of current figures available from public utilities (number of telephone installations, number electric meters, etc.), by using the same proportion of population to housing or other data as is indicated by the ratio in the preceding census.

Location vs. Site:

When making comparisons of locations, you are considering the site only as to its position relative to *other* sites, and not considering the site per se. Features such as topography, size, and shape, therefore, are site characteristics, and are not pertinent to analysis of the location itself.

Trends:

All data are significant to the particular appraisal problem only insofar as they can be analyzed for prediction, within a reasonable range of error, of future events. When using population, housing, or income data for establishment of trends of the future, absolute amounts are sometimes preferable to percentage amounts, for the base for a percentage change is itself altered each year in the same manner as compound interest.

Turning Statistics into Value Determinants:

All economic data of the community constitute the components of real estate value, as well as representing their particular statistical series. For this reason it is logical to use the statistical data in making comparisons, particularly between two different communities, as either a substitute or a supplement to market transactions.

As an example, suppose you need a rough estimate of a 100% land value in an unfamiliar city in which you have no sale data to give such an indication. A rough indication from statistical data may be derived as follows:

If a recent survey of "at work" population has been made for a subject city and for one in which you know the 100% land values, then this is the best possible indicator. This figure, however, is seldom available, but may in some cases be approximated by use of the employment data in the "Central Business Statistics" section of the Census of Business.

The following data will also serve to give a range of indications:

1. Population (city and Standard Metropolitan Statistical Area)
2. Population density (per square mile)
3. Total employment
4. Total sales
5. Retail sales (total and per household)

6. Median family (or per capita) income

7. Bank debits

8. Bank deposits

When these eight items for the subject property are tabulated, along with tabulations of the same figures for several cities in which the 100% value is known, the ratio of each to subject, as a percentage, may be derived. Application of this technique to 10 comparable cities will result in 80 indicators for subject, not all of them consistent, of course, but after analysis and narrowing to the most consistent indicators and ordering these data in an array, a pattern will begin to emerge so that a broad indication of the range of value sought may be derived from these data, all of which are available in published census statistics.

Census data are also useful in establishing broad levels of property values in residential areas. You will probably find, however, that comparisons based on median family income for particular census tracts are firmer than the actual estimates of value given in the census, as most respondents have a tendency to overestimate the value of their properties.

When reviewing an appraisal from another state, or from a city with which you are unfamiliar, census data furnish a great number of items which can be helpful in your review. For instance:

1. The general value range of residences in the neighborhood

2. Condition of the housing

3. Predominant age groups

4. Median incomes

5. Percentage of renter and owner occupancy

6. Type of employment

These data are also amenable to study by multiple regression analysis, which will be discussed later. Land value, or property value, or rent levels may be taken as the dependent variable, or answer sought, and the foregoing statistical data as the independent variables, or value determinants. The technique of regression analysis will be presented in Chapters XIV, XV, and XVI.

All of these factors are available in the census data, by census tract for all cities, and by individual blocks for larger cities. Data are also available for the central business districts of all larger cities.

When carefully analyzed, these figures are seen not to be mere dry statistics at all, but representative collections of data on the very "buyer and seller" postulated in your definition of value.

V

Market Analysis; Trending
Supply and Demand Elements;
Identifying the Buyer

The most common objective of a market analysis is to estimate the most probable sales volume of either an existing or proposed site use. On some occasions, a market analysis may be requested separately from an appraisal, but in the appraisal of any large commercial property, a market analysis of some sort should be included in the appraisal in order to establish a frame of reference for subsequent estimation of a specific market value for the property.

Market Analysis—Data Program:

The data program for such an analysis consists of a sample of the local market population, as to magnitude of population, median family income, family sizes, ages, and purchasing habits. Competitive properties must be spotted and the extent of competition estimated. Growth of the local economy with particular regard to "basic" land uses (commercial and industrial, or any export type of activities) must be projected.

The objective of such a study for industrial use will be either the amount of industrial land or of buildings which may be absorbed within a given period; for office and commercial uses, the amount of building space which may be absorbed within a given period; for stores, either free standing or shopping centers, the sales volume anticipated, and the consequent building area which will be supportable; for residential uses, the number of units in a given rental or price range that can be absorbed in a given period.

For commercial use, the supply and demand are estimated as to the amount of consumer expenditures to be captured by the subject property. The rate of space absorption must be estimated along with the estimated effective demand and available supply. For residential uses, the supply and demand for housing units, along with various income groups in the area, must be analyzed.

Commercial Property Analysis:

In making a market analysis for a commercial property, a shopping center or large free-standing store, the first step is the establishment of the primary trading area, as discussed in Chapter 3. Enumeration is then made of the number of families in this trading area and the amount of effective buying power or gross spendable income.

In the case of a proposed shopping center, the figures estimated relate to a period two to five years from the present, so some sort of population projection is necessary. Next, the amount of spendable income which may be captured by the subject property is estimated. This spendable income then is assigned to the various types of merchandise and services offered in the shopping center or store area.

Population:

Depending upon the time in which the study is made, and upon the local data available, the estimated population may be projected from the latest census data, when correlated with subsequent data from utility companies and/or building permits. In some cases, of course, it will be necessary to make an actual full count of homes in the accessible area.

Spendable Income:

This figure may be available in either the census data or *Sales Management's* "Survey of Buying Power." An alternative method, when published data are unavailable, is to investigate sale prices of homes in the subject area and convert these figures to the proportionate share of income which purchasers would typically spend for housing. The amount spent for housing is a rough indicator of spendable income per family.

Classification of Trade:

The merchandise and services offered may then be broken down, making reasonable allocations of expenditures for each classification of merchandise or services. At this point of the analysis great care is required in the study of competitive properties, as part of the drawing power of subject will have to come from these existing properties.

Analysis of spendable income, adjusted for the influence of available competition, and for the amount of through traffic which also may be captured by subject, will result in a final estimate of the total sales volume obtainable for the various classifications of goods and services offered.

Housing Market Analysis:

An analysis of the housing market for a community should contain the following:

1. Economic background of the area, particularly as to employment and income factors.
2. Definition of the area to which the study is applicable.
3. Supply factors
   a. Housing starts
   b. Demolitions and displacements
   c. Vacancies
   d. Sales and rental markets
   e. Public housing and urban redevelopment
4. Housing demand factors, both as to numbers of dwellings which can be absorbed by the market, and as to the price ranges needed.

Such an analysis will result in a final estimate of the quantity and quality of housing required for the particular housing area under study.

Industrial Properties:

In the analysis of industrial trends, emphasis will be shifted somewhat, focusing particularly on:

1. Zoning
2. Compatibility of uses
3. Availability of utilities
4. Accessibility to the various types of transportation
5. Raw material sources
6. Location of markets
7. Labor force

In projecting the future requirements of industrial building space, examine and classify the existing inventory as to whether the properties are actually available and/or competitive with subject. Future space requirements of the particular type are vital.

Industries whose product gains weight by processing will tend to locate nearer to their markets. Those whose product loses weight in processing will tend to locate nearer to their raw material sources.

Land Requirement Projection:

The following approach to establishment of future industrial land requirements was developed in "Industrial Land Needs Through 1980," by the Greater Boston Economic Study Committee:

Total number of acres used by industry equals

$$(Ei \times a) + (E_{mi} \times b) + (E_{me} \times c)$$

where

E_i	=	Intensive industry
E_{mi}	=	Moderately intensive industry
E_{me}	=	Moderately extensive industry

and where,

a	=	acres per worker used in intensive industry (E_i)
b	=	acres per worker used in moderately intensive industry (E_{mi})
c	=	acres per worker used in moderately extensive industry (E_{me})

The equation assumes that moderately intensive industrial use requires 1.5 x the land use required by intensive industries, while moderately extensive industries require 2.5 x as much land as the intensive industries. Based on the total estimated industrial employment, the required land may then be derived by substitution, as follows:

Total number of acres used by industry =

$$(E_i \times a) + (E_{mi} \times 1.5a) + (E_{me} \times 2.5a)$$

In the Boston study, for example, employment in intensive industry equaled 50,100. Employment in moderately intensive industry equaled 20,100. Employment in moderately extensive industry equaled 127,800 workers. 5,958 acres were used for manufacturing purposes at the time of the survey. From these data, the projected number of acres required per worker was made, based on present manufacturing land uses, as follows:

$(50.1a) + (20.1 \times 1.5a) + (127.8 \times 2.5a) = 5,958$		
a	=	14,904 acres per 1,000 workers
b	=	1.5a or (1.5 x 14,904) = 22,356 acres per 1,000 workers
c	=	2.5a or (2.5 x 14,904) = 37,260 acres per 1,000 workers.

The future land needs are then derived by applying the foregoing densities (number of acres required per 1,000 workers) to estimated future employment in the various industrial categories. These figures, multiplied by the number of acres per 1,000 workers results in the projected required land area.

Market Analysis—Motel or Hotel:

The following items are essential to this type of report:

1. Survey of economy of the area, as to population, industry, trade and services.
2. Transportation facilities, including highways, airlines, and rail facilities.

3. Survey of existing supply of hotel or motel units, with differentiation as to the units which are actually competitive with subject, and those which would not be competitive in the same market.

4. Effective demand for units including tourist and commercial trade and convention business. A study of the supply and demand over the few years preceding should result in a projection of the rate of absorption of this type of accommodation for the coming period.

Market Analysis—Office Building:

As in other markets, the office building market may be categorized as supply and demand elements.

Supply: The unit of measure for supply is net rentable area. An inventory must first be taken, of both occupied and vacant space. Terms of lease and types of tenants must be classified. The quality of the existing available areas must be compared with that of the proposed project, as much of the existing supply may not be competitive. The projected supply must be adjusted for the rate of demolition.

Demand: The objective of demand analysis is establishment of a projected absorption rate for new office space. Sources of demand are: (1) new firms, (2) expansion of existing facilities, (3) moves from old to new quarters, and (4) moves due to demolition.

Absorption of square footage of office space correlates to some extent with population growth, but the reliability of a single ratio of square footage per capita can vary widely, depending on the make-up of occupancies. In any projection, the timing of the proposed development must be considered.

New space required by growth of employment may be projected as follows:

(1) Establish ratio of office employees to total, and the space per employee.

(2) Determine employment in preceding years in finance, insurance, real estate, and service employment, and project the resulting trend.

(3) Apply the resulting ratio to the estimated future population. The difference between this estimate and the present employment gives the projected increase in office employment.

(4) Applying to this, the square footage per employee gives the office space required by expected population growth.

An adjustment in estimated demand is then made for possible future increase in the ratio of footage per employee.

Some demand will be generated by demolitions, but before these areas are simply added in, the *vacancy* rates prior to demolition should be investigated.

The rate of occupancy needed by the proposed office building may be derived by simply starting with the desired net return, and working an income approach in reverse, from net through expenses to the effective gross necessary to earn the given return. In projecting the marketability of such a property, it should be remembered that fine detail of expense analysis is all wasted if special care is not taken in establishing the two most crucial estimates: rental rate and vacancy rate.

Identifying the Buyer:

The proper definition of an appraisal problem does not depend entirely on the location of the property, but depends to a great extent on identification of a specific type of buyer. The property can be "worth" one amount to one purchaser and a different amount to another; the appraisal should reflect the particular client's needs.

Often the client himself merely assumes that he wants "an appraisal," meaning one specific value figure. You may have to define the problem for the client to ascertain what he really needs to know. This will be affected not only by the client's income tax position, but by his overall position with regard to other investments, the amount of his expertise regarding the particular property type, who will be handling the management, etc. When the client is not the prospective purchaser, the probable purchaser should be defined more sharply than has been done in the conventional appraisal process: a most probable tax bracket may be assumed, as well as financing ability, price range within which the probable investor will be operating, and his probable position respecting equity increment versus long-term return.

Market Causes and Effects:

It is often stated that commercial and industrial construction follow residential construction, and that population is the source of income and value. This, however, places cause and effect in exactly reverse order, and a competent appraiser cannot afford to confuse such issues in his analysis of a market.

A member of the population needs income, and thus employment, before he can buy a property. *Employment* is always the generative factor, not population. The population will come to the source of employment.

Effect of Financing on Modern
Appraisal Process

$\mathbf{M}$any of the definitions of market value in the past years have gone to considerable lengths to justify inclusion of the word "cash" in the defination, based on the assumption that market value consisted only of the price at which property would sell for all cash. It is clear, however, that a sale may be for all cash to the seller even though it is partially or totally financed by the purchaser (as in a VA sale).

Cash Value and Financed Value:

It is equally clear that in most markets the typical transaction involves financing of a substantial portion of the sale price. As a general rule, an appraisal should represent a price assuming typical, currently obtainable financing terms. Once the appraiser has recognized the financing and extracted the portion of the return assignable to debt service, then he has substantially reduced his possible range of error, as a large part of the value estimate has been removed from estimation and made a part of the factual data.

Financing Structure:

The financing on a property is made up of four variable items:

1. Rate of interest.
2. Ratio of loan to total value.
3. Terms of loan (in period of time).
4. Points, or discount in the current market of the mortgage.

When analyzing the financing of a property under appraisement, each of these four factors must be given separate consideration, both with respect to the subject property and, when possible, in comparison of the comparable properties with subject.

Effect of Ratio and Rate on Value:

It is often assumed that the overall capitalization and, therefore, the total property value, will vary with the mortgage-to-value ratio. As may be seen in the following illustration, however, this is not necessarily the case:

Financing, varying *ratio* only:

		Weighted Rate
Mtge.	.60 @ .06	.036
Equity	.40 @ .11	.044
		.080
Mtge.	2/3 @ .06	.040
Equity	1/3 @ .12	.040
		.080
Mtge.	.75 @ .06	.045
Equity	.25 @ .14	.035
		.080
Mtge.	.80 @ .06	.048
Equity	.20 @ .16	.032
		.080
Mtge.	.90 @ .06	.054
Equity	.10 @ .26	.026
		.080

As these computations indicate, a mortgage ratio can be increased to any amount, without necessarily affecting the overall capitalization rate, as the thinner the equity becomes, the higher the risk goes, and therefore, the higher return rate demanded on the equity. In this case, again, the fundamental theorem applies: Rate is approximately commensurate with risk.

As the equity ratio decreases, the rate of return of necessity also increases, because the thinner equity is accompanied by a higher risk.

Now let us begin with the same financing, varying mortgage rate only:

Mtge.	.60@ .06	.036
Equity	.40@ .11	.044
		.080
Mtge.	.60@ .07	.042
Equity	.40@ .095	.038
		.080
Mtge.	.60@ .08	.048
Equity	.40@ .08	.032
		.080
Mtge.	.60@ .09	.054
Equity	.40@ .065	.026
		.080

As shown in the second illustration, variation of the *interest rate* on the mortgage *does* have a bearing on the total overall capitalization rate.

In the illustration, the interest rate may be adjusted upward only two points (from 6% to 8%), to reach a level where the equity return is no higher than the mortgage return (holding the overall rate constant). When increased another point (to 9%) the equity rate to obtain the same overall return rate, would have to be lowered to 6.5% There would, of course, appear to be no point in an investor buying at this rate, since the mortgage position would carry a higher return than the equity position. There are some such transactions, however, sometimes due to miscalculation by the investor, and sometimes due to anticipated equity increment or attractive depreciation allowance.

Full Equity and Partial Equity:

An unencumbered, or full equity position is often less desirable than a partial equity.

An example of how financing can be used to increase a value is as follows:

A 34 unit apartment was producing collections of $22,500. A program of capital improvement was recommended, including a new boiler, rewiring, redecoration, carpets in public areas, exterior doors to apartments, replacing of lighting fixtures, for a total cost of $12,000.

The property was owned free and clear, with value "as is" being estimated at $83,000. It was suggested that the capital improvements be financed by a $15,000 loan, at 7.5% for a ten year period. The suggested capital improvements increased the income by $3,000 per year, showing a net profit to the total capital value of $20,000. The principal reason for the more desirable financial structure after financing was that the capital improvements could be installed with money costing a 7.5% interest rate, and would produce a real estate return as part of the total property at a rate of approximately 12%.

Non-Equity Properties:

As was graphically demonstrated by Roy Wenzlick,[1] the terms of a mortgage can be such as will result in no equity, not only at time of purchase, but for a long period thereafter. According to Wenzlick's chart, with a 40 year, no down payment loan, taking into account typical depreciation and cost of selling, a typical residence would require 21 years to achieve any equity position whatever. At any time prior to the 21st year, a purchaser would be assuming more liability on the mortgage than he would be receiving in property value.

This is primarily due to the long term and consequent minimal amortization of the mortgage. The appraiser and consultant's concern here is that low mortgage payments are not of necessity desirable, as they can reduce amortization to the point of diminishing return.

Methods of Financing:

There are a number of financing methods currently used, with which the appraiser should be familiar. Among these are the following:

1. Conventional first mortgage. Assuming financing of a shopping center:

   a.   Two-thirds of area and two-thirds of income normally must be derived from AAA-1 tenants.

   b.   All fixed charges (operating expenses, taxes, and debt service) must be covered by the income of the AAA-1's.

   c.   The financing of a large center can be shared by several lenders.

2. Sale-leaseback:

This type of transaction, in effect, supplies 100% financing for AAA-1 tenancy. The most favorable aspect of this transaction from the occupant's viewpoint is receipt of maximum financing, and he can charge the rental off as expense each year. The unfavorable aspect of this type of transaction is that the developer loses the depreciation allowance.

3. Separation of fee and leasehold:

On a long term leaseback, the land can be sold to the investor, and leased back to the builder. The investor simultaneously provides leasehold financing for the building.

Favorable aspects of this transaction from the developer's viewpoint is that more money is obtained, as the land is usually sold at approximately market value, compared with the 75% maximum obtainable when appraised as part of the total mortgage package. Carrying charges are less, as there is no amortization on the land. The land sale will generally be at 1-½% to 2% higher than the mortgage constant.

The builder is not faced with a problem of repurchasing the fee at a marked-up

---

1   *The Real Estate Analyst,* March 17, 1961.

price, and the lender gets a safe investment at 75% to 90% of value, well secured by the leasehold improvement. Carrying charges are less, being on building only. The developer gets total depreciation, as the ground rent and the interest payment are both fully deductible.

4. Leasehold financing:

If a leasehold is financed separately, the land being subordinated, ground rent is not deducted, and the mortgage figured the same as the fee interest. If the land is not subordinated, the lender determines whether the rent is fair and not too high in relation to the leasehold mortgage. The ground rent should not exceed two-thirds of one year's interest on the permanent mortgage. Generally, a leasehold mortgage will carry a higher interest rate than a conventional first mortgage, a shorter term, and a lower loan ratio.

5. Separate mortgaging of land and building is often useful. If the developer would have a high capital gains tax when selling land (where land was acquired on a low basis), he can mortgage it separately from the improvements: For example, a shopping center with very low land cost, with ground rent with renewal option. The unfavorable aspect of this transaction is less money obtainable by the developer. As a favorable factor, he retains the freedom to refinance.

6. Sale-buyback:

In a sale-buyback, or installment sales contract, the investor buys, selling back to the developer under terms of a long term installment contract. As the contract vendee has an interest in the title, he can take depreciation which he otherwise could not have under a sale leaseback.

The contract normally calls for a fixed contract payment, approximately equal to the prevailing mortgage constant for similar projects, plus a contingent payment based on the property's performance. The terms of this type of transaction are usually ten years longer than would be the case in a regular mortgage, thus increasing the investor's return over the life of the investment. The vendee is often granted a contract termination option which is the equivalent of prepayment privilege. The contingent payment may be a percentage of the net, less the contract payment.

On a sale-buyback for, say forty years, the builder or the developer can retain the right to buy back after ten or fifteen years, with a kicker, such as paying off the balance of the contract price. From the lender's point of view, he has a higher than normal basic interest rate or a re-purchase bonus, as well as a longer than normal closed option. An unfavorable aspect for the developer is that he has a partner sharing the profits of the development. An unfavorable aspect to the lender is the high risk factor because of higher than normal investment.

7. Basket Money:

Maximum financing is often obtained by use of "basket money." This is a portion of a lender's funds which he is permitted to use at his discretion, and which would otherwise not meet the legal requirements for his mortgages. Some of the types of financing available under this clause are:

a.   A first mortgage exceeding the legal rate.

b.   Second mortgages.

c.   Wrap-around mortgages.

d.   Mortgage and sale-leaseback of subordinated fees.

e.   Subordinated convertible debentures.

f.   Loans secured by leases but not by mortgages.

g.   Front money, or participation in equity.

Such participation may consist of a percentage of gross income, of net income, or of equity. The percentage clause often amounts to an even higher financing cost than appears at first glance. For example, a recent mortgage on a new restaurant property was for 10.5% interest, on a 75% ratio ($105,000), plus 0.5% of gross income. This 1/2%, however, when converted to dollars on the basis of the restaurant's projected sales ($420,000), amounts to 2% of the mortgage, resulting in a constant of 13.98%.

The appraiser has two choices as to processing participations in his valuation: by adding to the mortgage interest rate, or by deducting from income. In my opinion, the latter is the proper procedure. In addition to the basic principle of arithmetic, that a denominator factor in the value equation should not be adjusted to account for changes in the numerator, another consideration applies: Adjustments to the mortgage interest rate will create errors in any after-tax cash flow projections, and in the amount of interest expense. For instance, in the foregoing example, calling the interest rate 12.5% would distort the amount of interest and amortization while in fact, the amortization would not be affected at all. The $2,100, therefore, should simply be deducted from the income, as it is really the equity whose value must be estimated. The capitalization rate has not been affected; the amount of equity income has.

One institution currently offers financing at 10 1/8%, for 25 years, plus 25% of future rent increases after a 5% vacancy allowance. As is often the case, prepayment is closed for 10 years, with prepayment penalty then of 5%, decreasing 1% per year. With this sort of financing, great care must be taken in projecting the expectable future income received by the equity owner.

When rising, declining, or fluctuating income is anticipated, the income should be projected year by year, the participation factor applied, and each year's adjusted income discounted separately.

8.   Often the investor (lender) has a first call on the property's cash flow until his investment is recovered, plus an agreed upon return, whereupon he and the developer become 50-50 partners. Or the investor may own the fee interest, while the builder-partner owns the leasehold. In this case the developer-partner receives all depreciation and can pay the investor his 50% interest as tax deductible ground rent.

9.   Bond Issues:

Financing may be obtained through bond issues, in which the lender will require a completely net lease from high credit tenants, and sufficient rent to amortize the loan within the terms of the lease. The interest rate and terms depend on the tenant's net worth and financial stability.

10. Gap financing:

Gap, or interim financing is used for the construction period, during which time the maker of the permanent financing has a hold-back portion which is larger than the amount of cash equity the developer can produce.

In this case, the secondary lender furnishes a stand-by commitment, so that the permanent lender may provide the additional take-out for the construction lender, and the full amount of the maximum available permanent loan may be borrowed, rather than stopping at the floor of the permanent loan commitment.

11. Variable rate mortgage:

Under this type of mortgage an entire commitment may be patterned to fit the income levels expected by the purchaser. The payments may increase, decrease, or remain level for certain periods of time. This type of financing is peculiarly fitted to follow the expectable income of a young junior executive with increasing salary anticipated, and for older persons nearing retirement age and whose income may be expected to decline. This type of mortgage, though seldom used at present, may be expected to become more common, especially when one considers that it only requires a few minutes more arithmetic calculations than the usual constant payment mortgage. The consultant can be of greater service to his client by selecting the most advantageous payment pattern.

Purchase Option:

Many leases, of course, are drawn up with options to purchase. When there is any likelihood of a prior option being exercised, particularly in the case of service station property, it is necessary to check the record out on the transaction, as the apparently current transaction may represent only the exercising of an option set ten or fifteen years earlier, at a time when the present value of the property was unanticipated.

Land Contract Sales:

Land contract sales are often used in sales of inexpensive houses to purchasers with little or no down payment and with questionable ability to meet the monthly payment. The first thing the appraiser needs to ascertain, when using these transactions as comparable sales, is the actual date of the meeting of the minds, as the deed is only recorded after the property is paid for, so that the actual sale price may have been set ten years ago or more.

Usually, with this type of transaction, a secondary market exists in which these land contracts can be sold, at discounts of anywhere from 15% to 30%. Since the contract is not convertible to cash at its full value, it appears that the market value of a property sold in this manner would consist of the equity (if any) or down payment, plus the discounted value in the secondary market of the land contract.

Discount Points:

When "points" are deducted from the face value of a mortgage, the net result from the lender's viewpoint is to raise the effective interest rate to the level of the market. The unrealistic control of mortgage interest rates lower than the market rate for such risks, often results in purchasers actually paying more effective interest than if the nominal interest rate had been allowed to follow the market. The amount of accounting and administrative work is also increased by the use of points, which further increases the cost of the mortgage.

From the appraiser's viewpoint, what the mortgagor does with his mortgage money is irrelevant; in this case, he has paid part of it for financing expenses. Face of the mortgage, rate and ratio remain the same. Attempting to adjust the interest rate would distort the interest and amortization ratios in any cash flow projection. Moreover, the points may reflect risk rating of the mortgagor, and have no valid relationship to the property.

Equity and the Entrepreneurial Factor:

Many persons, including appraisers, lenders, and brokers, have based their analyses of properties on the implicit assumption that the value consisted of the land cost plus the building cost. Appraisers have come to recognize, however, that a third factor, that of the entrepreneurial profit, is a portion of the property's value to an investor. The thinner the cash equity, the more crucial this factor becomes.

In "The Appraisal Journal" of the American Institute of Real Estate Appraisers, October 1963, Sanders A. Kahn demonstrated the need for recognition of entrepreneurial profit as a factor in total property value. The purpose here is to discuss an actual example from the market, and to draw conclusions as to one approach to measurement of this factor. Familiarity with Dr. Kahn's basic concept is assumed.

Example:

The sale property is a two story brick veneer apartment, 12 units, average construction. There are four 3-bedroom units renting at $95, and eight 2-bedroom units at $80, or Gross Annual Rental of $12,240, no utilities furnished. The lot is 93 x 313, in a fair location.

After deduction of vacancy allowance and operating expenses, the net annual rental was estimated at $8,400. Total cost of the project to the entrepreneur, including building contractor's profit, was $82,500. Indicated Gross Annual Multiple, therefore, for the entrepreneur was 6.74. Overall net rate of return was 10.2%.

The property was sold as an investment for $99,300, with the entrepreneur "mortgaging out." Overall net rate of return was 8.5%. The entrepreneur's profit was 20.4%.

Comments:

1.   The problem here as to "what is the value" or "what is the cost" is analogous to the question as to what is the cost of a house, which is generally agreed to consist of, not the cost to the builder, nor even the cost of land plus contractor's cost

and profit, but the cost to the ultimate purchaser, so that the cost of improvements may be most easily and correctly found, by simply subtracting the indicated land value from the sale price of the house-and-lot package. Similarly, the entrepreneur's service in packaging the going property is a part of cost new, whether he has recovered it in dollars or not.

2. The appraiser's analysis should not be confused by any consideration of whether the entrepreneur happens to "mortgage out":

a. If market value is the objective, and if the applicable rate of return for an *investor,* and the resultant indicated value for investor are consistent with the market, his problem is solved.

b. If, however, he is pricing a proposed package for an entrepreneur, he uses the higher entrepreneur's rate, or reduces the "cost new" by the indicated percentage. As in the example, if investor's value or probable selling price were determined, and the entrepreneur's warranted cost were the objective of the appraiser's analysis, then $99,300/120.4% = $82,500, the warranted cost to the entrepreneur.

3. The equity dividend for entrepreneur and that for investor can vary much more than the overall rate of return, especially as the entrepreneur may have little or actually no equity except for the entrepreneurial service itself.

4. If a number of such examples in the market are analyzed, then, when the cost of a particular project is known, the appraiser can refer to a file of good indicators of the percentage factor of profit which has been realized by entrepreneurs involved in putting together the particular type and size of property, so that these percentage factors can be used in converting a known cost to investor's value. Conversely, when a proposed selling price to an investor is known, this can be converted to the warranted cost to an entrepreneur.

5. In estimating value of property which is still in the hands of an entrepreneur, the criterion of market value is the *investor's* rate. The two functions, of entrepreneur and investor, operate at different levels of risk. They should always be recognized as separate functions, with each assigned its proper rate, even though in particular instances the two functions often happen to be performed by the same person.

The investor who is well informed, but either unable or unwilling to perform the entrepreneur's function, obviously considers the entrepreneur worthy of his hire, since he was willing to put, in the example, $16,800 into the cash equity position as compensation for the entrepreneurial factor.

Conclusions:

Financing techniques are constantly becoming more sophisticated. The appraiser must keep himself well informed on these developments, as the particular financing method anticipated may make a considerable difference in the valuation process. The mortgage portion of the capital structure should always be removed from the valuation problem, by determining what part of the return is attributable to debt service. (The Ellwood Process, which synthesizes a rate of return from equity and mortgage analysis, will be treated separately in Chapter XIII.)

The appraiser can enhance his utility to the client by explicitly furnishing the varying warranted prices indicated under differing given financial structures of a proposed purchase or development.

In the appraisal report, the section discussing the financing technique appropriate for the subject property should come after the marketability discussion, and before the valuation section, as the financing, in the same manner as the neighborhood and marketability sections, is one of the factors which go to make up the total complex of value determinants.

VII

Location Analysis and
Site Valuation

In the analysis of a location and valuation of a site, the focus of the appraiser's study is narrowed successively from the region, to the community, to the specific site.

Highest and Best Use:

Treatment of the detailed highest and best use study will be found in Chapter XVII. Since any type of appraisal, however, implies some analysis of the highest and best use, attention is directed at this point only to the following major factors:

1. The study should include an analysis of the area economics and analysis of the markets for housing, retail, hotel or motel, office space, or parking space.
2. The types and the intensity of urban uses which will be marketed in the location are determined.
3. A projection is made of the absorption rate for each type of marketable use.
4. The land areas and approximate siting for the various uses are allocated.

5. Staging of the proposed development is estimated.

6. The economic feasibility is analyzed.

7. Value of the land is estimated, discounting for deferred uses, if appropriate.

Industrial Location Factors:

It may appear that more emphasis is placed on industrial location analysis than on any other type of property use. The reason is that this type of analysis is required more often for industrial locations than for other property types, the locations of the majority of other land uses more often being already determined before the appraiser or consultant is called in. An approach to this type of analysis should cover the following steps:

Region:
1. Labor force
2. Employment
3. Income
4. Population
5. Economic background and growth rate of the area
6. Transportation
7. Trend of land usage
8. Geographical factors
9. Financial institutions
10. Local government attitudes and tax structures
11. Cultural and recreational facilities
12. Construction costs

Community:
13. Geography
14. Local markets
15. Transportation (methods and costs)
16. Community services and facilities
17. Compatibility of land uses
18. Utilities
19. A more detailed analysis of population than was required at the regional level as to age groups, race, sex, education
20. Labor supply

Site Factors:

The following is a checklist of industrial site factors from "Methods of Plant Site Selection," Small Business Administration. These factors, of course, are important for either small or large plants.

1. Size and shape of lots
2. Topography
3. Availability and cost of utilities
4. Water supply
5. Possibility of flooding
6. Drainage
7. Soil conditions
8. Cost of development
9. Location in community
10. Transportation facilities
11. Fire and police protection
12. Taxes and insurance
13. Zoning and other legal aspects
14. Suitability of existing building
15. Price

Attention is directed to the fact that the price of the land is the last item considered. Considering the total investment in a new plant facility, the price of the site is such a small proportionate part of the investment as to rate very low in final consideration of the important and relevant factors. Moreover, additional site costs are often necessary, such as: grubbing, stripping, dock-height fill, piling, back fill, cuts, rock blasting, connecting with utility lines.

Least-Cost Distribution Point:

As a preliminary step in the siting of an industrial facility, determination of the least-cost distribution point is a good indication of the region within which to select the most desirable location.

The following application is adapted from "Methods of Plant Site Selection Available to Small Manufacturing Firms," prepared by West Virginia University for the Small Business Administration. Assume a plant in Alabama, whose raw material sources are Birmingham, Gadsden, Huntsville, and whose markets are in Tuscaloosa, Mobile, Montgomery, Dothan, and Phenix City–Columbus.

The company wants to relocate, with the major factor being determination of the point at which their costs of distribution (importation of raw materials and exportation of finished products) are the lowest.

The problem is analyzed as follows (see Figure 7.1):

1.   Trace a map of the total area under consideration including all of the company's material sources and markets.

2.   Locate these transport points on the map, identifying each location by letter or other symbol.

3.   Draw an X line (horizontal), and a Y line (perpendicular) on the map, so as

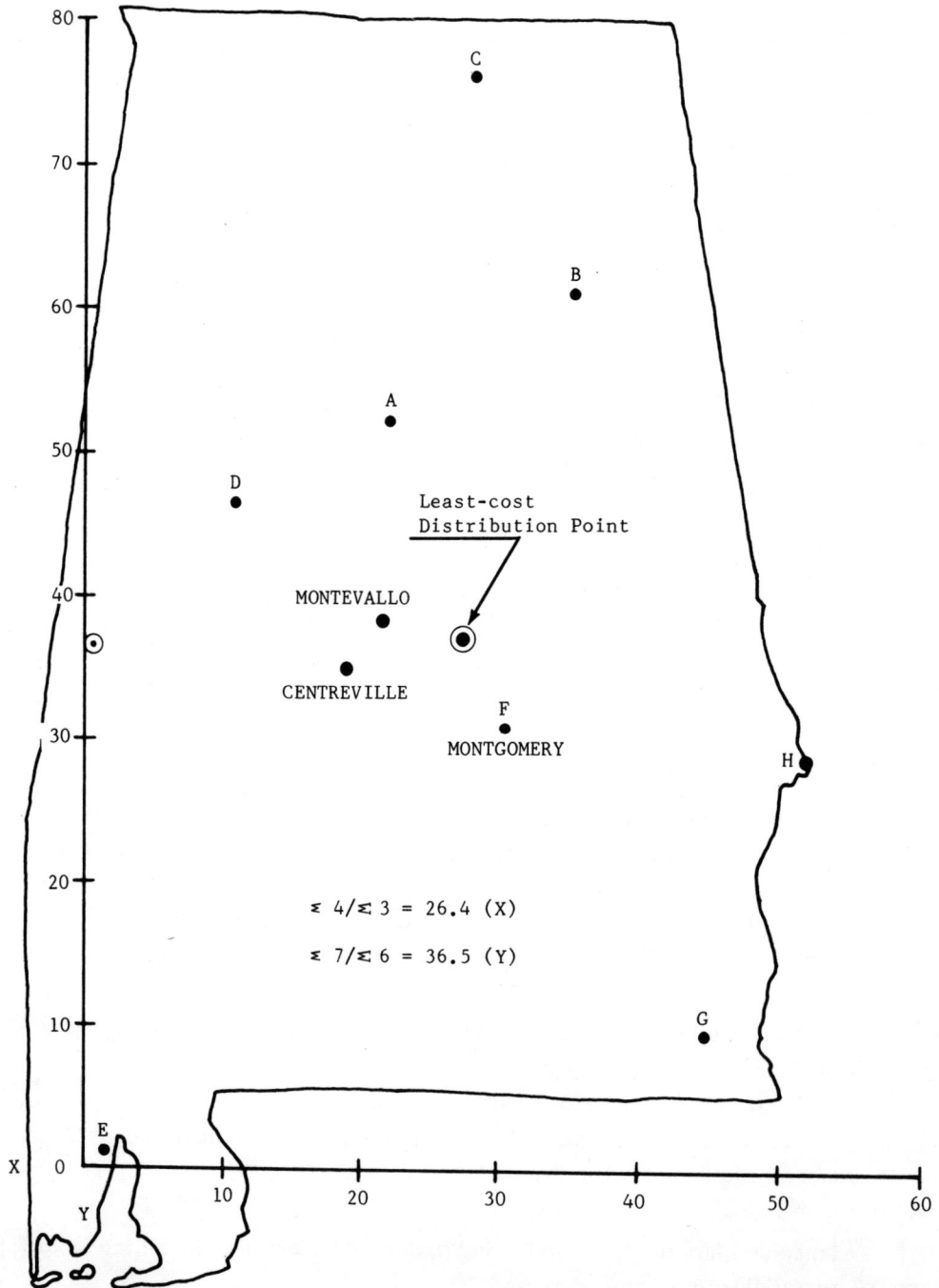

Figure 7.1 Least-Cost Distribution Point

to include all of the material and market points within the two lines. The map should be drawn on graph paper, or X and Y lines simply numbered and kept in scale.

4. Prepare a table listing the material sources and markets. Next, identify each location by its X and Y numbers listing these across the table as shown.

5. Tabulate first the X units, reading from the left side of the table, across to the locations; then the tonnage weights of shipping from the material sources. Multiply these two factors.

6. Then list Y units (reading from the bottom left of scale, upward to the location); and the tonnage weights for these locations. Multiply these two factors in the last column.

7. The tonnage figures for the market locations should be adjusted for differing transportation cost for raw materials and finished products. In this case, we are assuming that the transportation cost for the finished product is twice that for the raw materials. Therefore, the tonnage weights of these shipments are simply doubled in the table. Any differential in freight costs may be compensated for in this way.

8. The balance of this computation is the simple arithmetic of completion of the table, giving a weighted average for each of the X and Y points.

9. The least-cost distribution point is located by counting to the right of the horizontal axis the number of spaces equal to the weighted average value of X. From this point, count vertically along the Y axis, the number of spaces equal to the weighted average value of Y. The point of intersection is the "ideal", or least-cost distribution point. Encircle this point.

10. A larger circle may then be drawn around this spot to indicate the general area to be investigated. In the example, the least-cost point is located in an area which may be considered to include Montgomery, Montevallo, and Centreville.

This technique, of course, does not necessarily determine the ideal spot for a relocation, but gives a good indication of the lowest transport cost area, within which to search for suitable communities and sites.

In the example it would be suggested that preliminary investigations be made as to sites in the three most likely communities, followed by analysis of these communities to determine the specific location most desirable for the particular facility, considering all of the industrial "checklists" cited above. Montgomery would appear to be the most likely choice for the company's new location.

| (1) | (2) | (3) | (4) | (5) | (6) | (7) |
| | X | Tonnage | 2 x 3 | Y | Tonnage | 5 x 6 |
Material Sources	Units	Weights		Units	Weights	
(A) Birmingham	23	40	920	53	40	2,120
(B) Gadsden	36	20	720	56	20	1,120
(C) Huntsville	29	10	290	76	10	760
Markets						
(D) Tuscaloosa	12	30	360	47	30	1,410
(E) Mobile	2	20	40	1	20	20
(F) Montgomery	31	40	1,240	26	40	1,040
(G) Dothan	46	20	920	9	20	180
(H) Phenix City-Columbus	53	10	530	29	10	290
		190	5,020		190	6,940

Site Analysis:

The site factors of intensity and density should be distinguished as follows:

1. Density of use relates to the coverage of the land with building. The use is not necessarily intensive, even though possibly located in the center of the central business district.
2. Intensity of use relates to a high generative capacity. Examples are service stations, branch banks, hamburger shops.

The following industrial site factors, in descending order of importance, were derived from a survey of broker members of the Society of Industrial Realtors, and corporate real estate executives, by Robert E. Boblett, MAI-SIR:

OF MAJOR SIGNIFICANCE:
1. Markets
2. Labor
3. Transportation
4. Raw materials

OF SECONDARY SIGNIFICANCE:
5. Availability of suitable sites
6. Character of city
7. Adequacy of water, sewer, etc.
8. Presence of supporting facilities
9. Tax climate
10. Local government reputation
11. Suitable housing for labor and management

OF THIRD LEVEL SIGNIFICANCE:
12. Cultural aspects of the city

13. Availability of suitable building or buildings
14. Quality of police and fire protection
15. Climate
16. Proximity to owner's home
17. Special inducements

The relative rank of Item # 17 should be of special interest to the appraiser serving as consultant to municipalities initiating programs of industry-hunting.

Residential Subdivision Land:

The following is a general guide to the factors considered in comparison of sites proposed for residential subdivision development:

1. Zoning, restrictions, protective covenants
2. Position of neighborhood relative to the other functional areas of the city, especially employment centers, recognizing, however, that the concept of complete homogeneity being inherently good and heterogeneity inherently bad, is no longer tenable (excellent examples are Columbia and Reston).
3. Character of neighboring developments
4. Physical and social appeal
5. Adequacy of civic, social, and commerical centers
6. Local government and governmental services
7. Medical and hospital services
8. Taxes, special assessments, liens on title
9. Relative marketability
10. Land acquisition and development costs

Each of these factors, of course, may be broken down in actual practice to a number of subfactors. The foregoing, therefore, is intended as a general guide only.

Office Site:

Analysis of location for office building development may proceed generally along these lines:

1. Establishment of effective demand for new space in the area, present absorption rate, and projected future demand.
2. Projections of space occupied by major categories of users.
3. Supportable rate structure for the office space.
4. Amount and type of parking required, and parking costs.
5. Economic feasibility, analyzed as to: cost and rent ranges, and income, expense and cash flow analysis, with indication of net return on the total investment.

Hotel or Motel Sites:

Prior to estimation of value of a specific site for this use and/or prior to development, the following factors should be investigated:

1. Total number of guest rooms that the market would support.
2. Sources of guest patronage.
3. Probable rate structure.
4. Suggested supporting recreational and other facilities.

Pricing Units—Land:

Apartments—Apartment sites are generally priced by the price per unit built on the site, and the price per square foot of land. A less commonly used unit of comparison, but one which is becoming of more utility as land use controls become more common, is the price per square foot of building.

A fourth pricing unit, and one which I have found to be more consistent and logical than either of the others, is the price *per dollar of gross rent.* To obtain this pricing unit, we simply divide the price paid by the gross possible rent. The ratio will, of course, vary from one community to another, but it has been my observation that this price falls within a much narrower range than the other pricing units, with the prices virtually all falling within the range of $ .80 to $1.20 *per dollar of gross rent.* In view of the prevalent use of gross annual multiples in pricing the *total* apartment project, it is just as logical to price the *land* in this manner. This pricing unit achieves a high degree of consistency, as it gets closer than the other pricing units to the land value reflected by the income residual to the land.

Commercial Land—Commercial land may be priced by virtually any of the foregoing units, with the addition of two further pricing units: The price per front foot is often used in areas of very high commercial land values, and where frontage is the principal commodity being purchased.

The other pricing unit for this type of land is the "chunk" method, that is, comparing total site with total site. The importance of the latter may be seen, for example, with respect to service station sites, in which the price per front foot is a better criterion than the price per square foot, as long as the lot has a useable depth. The site, however, is a more accurate criterion than the price per front foot.

The reason for the desirability of at least a review of the overall site prices may be noted in the great number of individual value determinants going to make this composite price. There is not, for instance, one traffic count at a simple two-street intersection, but a minimum of *twelve* (straight ahead, left, or right, for each of four streets).

Industrial Land—Industrial land is usually priced on the basis of square footage, but in peculiar situations where the amount of building is limited, comparisons are sometimes better made by way of the price per square foot of allowable building on site.

Residential—Residential lots are often priced by the front foot, but the principal reason for doing so is that the appraiser is filling out a form or following an instruction which asks for this figure. Actually, a residential site can be intelligently compared only on a *per site* basis, often referred to as the "chunk" method. The reason for this is that, regardless of front footage, there are only two possible numbers of sites involved: the lot furnishes one building site or two building sites.

Land Value Map—When presenting the valuation of unusually large tracts of land, or those with several frontages or several possibilities for division, a land value map, shown in Figure 7.2, is helpful to the reader of the report in visualizing the value conclusion. Such a map does not imply that the values are assigned separately for each square foot or front foot involved or for uneconomic divisions of the total tract, but is merely for the purpose of showing a reasonable allocation of the overall land value, so that the appraisal reviewer or client can more easily check the comparability of the sale properties and test their relevance to the land valuation problem at hand.

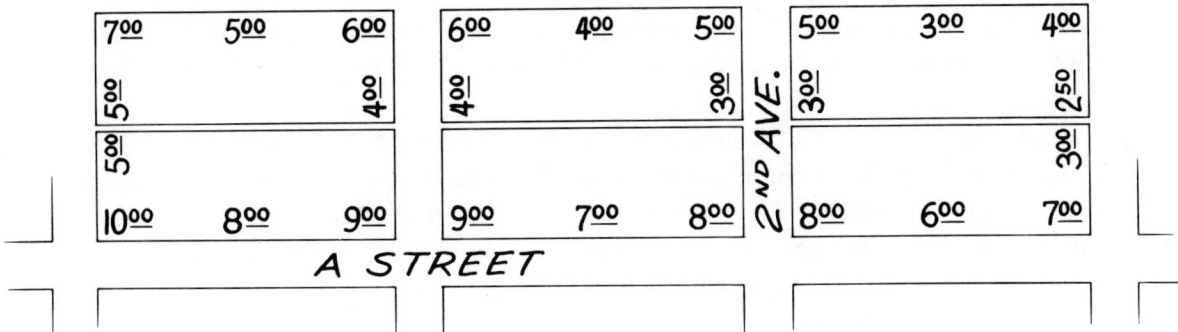

Figure 7.2 Land Value Map

Comparable Sale Adjustments:

Since the reader's familiarity with the basic elements of appraising is assumed, discussion will be confined to those sales adjustments which are most often misused.

Accessibility:

This adjustment does *not* consider the comparable in its relation to other properties. It *does* include consideration of: traffic arteries, (truck, auto, bus), corners, alleys, (side or rear), one-way streets, railroad trackage, traffic light placement, traffic flow pattern.

Size and Shape:

This adjustment may be broken down, depending upon the degree of similarity of comparable properties and subject property, into several factors: size, shape, width, depth, plottage, and range of economic size.

In considering the width of a comparable sale lot with that of subject, note that in most cases excess width over the basic lot size sells at a considerably reduced unit price, until the point is reached at which the width becomes sufficient for a second lot.

In considering the depth, as well as shape, the most important factor involved is usually the relation of frontage to area, modified by analysis of the overall utility of the total tract.

In making comparisons of large acreage tracts, a useful criterion is the front feet per acre. After a norm is established for a particular area, a large deviation, whether up or down, calls for an adjustment for this factor.

Corner Influence—Commercial:

Corner influence factors are often computed by the application of a per front foot value of the side street, considering the side street as additional frontage, and considering the front or main street as the depth of the lot to obtain a corner influence factor. It is much simpler, however, and as accurate, to handle corner influence as follows:

As lot sales are accumulated and posted to maps and filed in the data file, hold out any sale which is either a corner with inside sales posted close to it, or, conversely, an inside lot sale in a block in which you have a corner lot sale posted. By making allowance for the time of sale, and any other differentiating factors, the corner influence may be quite simply expressed as a single percentage figure, added to the unit land value of the inside lot.

If these inside and corner sales are regularly posted, it will be found that a percentage for corner influence in a particular section of the city and for specific uses begins to fall within a very narrow range. Allowance must be made, of course, for premium purchases of adjoining properties by expanding companies, etc. This single adjustment for corner influence as against the attempt to compute a side street as frontage, and the front street as depth for the side street, is simpler in application, more provable in the market, and more easily comprehensible to a jury.

This process may be considerably refined by application of multiple regression analysis, whereby the value contribution of corner influence, or any other value determinant, may be isolated. This valuation approach will be discussed in Chapter XV.

Corner Influence—Residential Lot:

A corner influence factor is often applied to residential lots. A study of actual sales in the area, however, will indicate that in most cities, there is no premium assignable to the corner location of residential lots. For example, a study of several thousand lot sales in the Birmingham (Ala.) area disclosed no justification for a corner influence factor in the residential lot market.

In cases where corner lots sold for higher prices than inside lots, there was always some other factor to account for the difference, such as a better view, larger lot, or landscaping.

The major source of the concept of residential corner influence was the fact that many years ago in small towns, the houses and combined offices, of the doctor, pastor, and later, lawyer, were located on corners in the most accessible, prominent locations in the town. The reason for additional premium for these corner residential lots, however, was simply that they were only partly residential, being partly the equivalent of commercial lots, as prominent locations were desirable for the particular professional occupancy. With the exception of row housing, however, the application of this factor at the present time is, in most cities, completely contrary to the market evidence.

Plottage:

An analysis of sales of commercial lots of varying sizes will, in most locations, indicate that, other factors being equal or equated by adjustments, the *unit* sale price of a commercial lot goes down as the land area increases. This conclusion, derived from sale data, is a direct contradiction of the concept of plottage value. It is generally borne out in the market, however, when premium purchases made under duress by adjoining owners are eliminated from the study, so as only to compare large lots with small lots.

When plottage increment is found to accrue, it will in most cases be found to exclude benefits of the corner influence element, as the land usages benefiting from plottage normally obviate simultaneous usages which benefit from corner influence.

The extent, and even the existence, of this factor depends on the typical, or normal building site size, for the specific city or neighborhood under study. The principal reason for the general impression of the rigid application of this factor may be attributed mainly to the fact that much early appraisal literature originated in the city of New York, in which there are a great number of tiny lots, so that this factor actually does exist in this and several other of the largest cities. In cities, however, where the typical lot sizes are 50 x 140, or 100 x 240, a plottage factor is seldom encountered in the market.

The appraiser should always approach with some skepticism any categorical dicta in any appraisal literature, including the present work. Many rules laid down as general statements are only partially applicable, or totally inapplicable, to a specific area at a specific time.

The appraiser or consultant, therefore, should not be afraid to change the rules when such changes are indicated in the marketplace. Always defer to the marketplace: money is still smarter than appraisers.

VIII

Sale Data and the Sale Comparison Approach

The value of a thing was defined by Matheson[1] in 1884 as "that which it will fetch." Since then, appraisers have invented and revised numberless definitions of value, and still find that the most usual solution to be sought in a particular valuation problem is simply "what will it sell for?"

The major modifications of this basic definition of value may be reduced to one concept: placement within a context. This would include the propositon, as expressed by Babcock, that there is not *the* value, but *a* value, which is to say, value for a given use, under given circumstances. It is now also recognized by most thoughtful appraisers that there is a value to a particular person or firm. Another modification recognizes that the value estimate is not an exact figure, but that, within the given context there is a most probable estimate; a probable range of prices, and that the degree of probability is measurable.

What Is the Market?

For purposes of valuation, the market may be defined as all of the options or alternatives available to the assumed purchaser or seller.

[1] Ewing Matheson, *The Depreciation of Factories* (3rd edition; London: E. & F. N. Spon, Ltd., 1903), p. 111.

The appraiser's problem is always to substitute and compare the seller-buyer's alternatives. Suppose you have a "comparable sale" at $100,000: under many circumstances, if a gross annual multiple of nine is indicated, isn't rental at $11,000 per year also a satisfactory substitute property? Or, if an overall net return of 8 percent is indicated, isn't a property with $8,000 net rental also a comparable?

Marketability:

Before a dollar figure can be assigned to the property, it must first be established whether it is marketable at all or not. If the answer is affirmative, then some form of measurement should be applied to this marketability. This may take the form of a rate of absorption of units of the particular type of property per year, or changes in value which may be reasonably anticipated under changing conditions, or, simply a definite estimate of the "reasonable time to find a purchaser" posited either explicitly or implicitly in all value definitions.

In the same manner as the value estimate itself, this estimate may be expressed as a range, which is valid only for the particular property type, and varying from one area to another.

For investment properties, the supply and demand elements of the market should be analyzed, as discussed in Chapter IV. In the report, this analysis should precede the discussion of specific comparable sales, as this is the economic base from which the specific sales arise.

Why One Approach?

The basic principle supporting the concept of all usable economic data being part of the "market" approach, is simply that there is no relevant experience with respect to the property under appraisement, until something happens, somewhere, to something in the marketplace. It is only there, in the meeting of two minds and agreement upon the indifference figure at which a transaction will occur, that data are generated which are pertinent to the appraisal process.

Pricing Units—Improved Properties:

Residential—In the appraisal of single family residences, only two units of comparison have proved to be of utility:

1. "The chunk," that is, a total price, plus lump sum dollar adjustments.

2. Price per square foot of livable area, including land. In using this unit of comparison, the sale price of the comparable property is simply divided by the livable area of the house. This comparison unit, with allowances made for basements, air conditioning, garages, etc., is particularly useful in studies analyzing a large quantity of data, such as an entire residential subdivision. When a sizable number of residential sales have been tabulated by price per square foot, the "double contract" and other non-arm's length transactions stand out in clear relief, for the base price per square foot of livable area is

normally quite consistent within a subdivision or any other natural neighborhood grouping.

Apartments—Apartments have five basic pricing units: the price per unit, per room, per square foot of building including land, gross annual multiple, and net return.

The price per unit is seldom very illuminating unless the properties being compared are virtually identical, since a unit may consist of anything from one room with common bath to six or eight rooms and two or three baths.

The price per room is considerably more accurate and consistent than the price per rental unit as the price is reduced nearer to a common denominator.

The price per square foot of building is a further refinement, but has the same weakness as the preceding two pricing units, in that the size and quality and, for that matter, all other descriptive data, can vary to great extremes.

The gross annual multiple is the most widely used comparison unit by both appraisers and investors, even for extremely expensive projects. This pricing unit has greater consistency, as many otherwise necessary adjustments are automatically accounted for in the rent itself.

The fifth pricing unit, net return, expresses the relationship between the earnings and total price of the property. It does *not* necessarily predict an economic life or even the future income, but merely expresses a current ratio between the two factors.

Commerical—There are four generally used pricing units for improved commercial property: the price per square foot of building including land, the price per front foot of land including building, the gross annual multiple, and the net return rate.

The price per square foot of building is often usable, but has the same weaknesses as it has in apartment appraisals.

The price per front foot of land including building is most usable in the close-in and downtown areas, particularly where the land values constitute a large proportion of the total property values. When a sufficient quantity of data has been accumulated on commercial properties, net return rates may be derived for those on which this figure has been unobtainable by dividing the gross annual multiple by the indicated net operating ratio.

Industrial Properties—Industrial properties are most commonly compared by the price per square foot of building including land. When pricing on this basis, the appraiser should always note the great importance of the land coverage ratio. The other two common pricing units for industrial properties are the gross annual multiple, and the net return rate.

Basic Unit for Income Properties:

A review of the foregoing pricing units, and consideration of any other the appraiser may use indicates that the one pricing unit most consistently recurring and which may be considered the basic pricing unit for income properties is the overall net return rate, or earnings/price ratio. This rate may then be adjusted for comparability with the subject property with as few adjustments as possible, which can include the following:

1. Market. This factor includes the time element, as time alone is of no significance except insofar as it alters market conditions. This factor would reflect changes in interest rates and prices, velocity and magnitude of market activity and changes in supply and demand.
2. Quality and duration of income.
3. Amenity factors.
4. Motivation (buyer and seller).

These four adjustments all have an element of subjectivity, but they can be monetized in the rate applied to the subject property. Adjustments should not be attempted in less than 1/8% fractions, as the market would not evaluate these factors finer than 1/8%.

For example, with a sale indicating a 9% return:

1. Interest rates up ½%; allowing for lag of effect and for portional effect on total property, rate is adjusted upward ¼%.
2. Quality: Subject has a higher rated tenant; adjusted downward 1/8%.
3. Amenity: Subject is inferior, comparable having a prestigious location; adjusted upward 1/8%.
4. Motivation: Similar in both cases, no adjustment. Net indication for subject 9 ¼%.

The appraiser should always remember that not all income properties are purchased for their income alone. Purchase for reasons other than net return, though, do not negate the relationship between earnings and price indicated by the sale, and do not negate the validity of the transaction. For example, the purchase of an income property primarily for the income tax loss obtainable by the purchaser does not mean that the sale is no good, nor is a sale at auction, or a transaction between members of a family, necessarily invalid. These situations merely mean that care must be taken in analyzing and adjusting for sale motivation.

Comparable Sale Adjustments:

In adjusting comparable sales, the ideal is obvious: The best adjustment is no adjustment. Exact similarity of the comparable property to subject would greatly mitigate the valuation problem, but, given the unique location and attributes of every property, an unadjusted identity is highly improbable.

The logic applicable to comparable sale adjustments was once stated concisely by Whitehead: "We habitually observe by the method of difference." He went on to illustrate, "Sometimes we see an elephant, and sometimes we do not. The result is that an elephant, when present, is noticed." This is precisely the appraiser's process: find comparable properties as similar to subject as possible, then forget the similarities and analyze the dissimilarities. His basic questions regarding comparable and subject are:

(1) What are the differences? (2) Then, how to monetize the differences? Since the differences which the appraiser seeks to identify and monetize are not always as easily noticeable as elephants, difficulties occasionally arise.

Time of Sale—A single adjustment to sale price for the time of sale, adjusting the transaction to current market conditions, cannot properly be applied to all properties generally in a given community. This adjustment can apply correctly only to (1) the given neighborhood, (2) the given property type, and often (3) the specific property.

A time of sale adjustment may quite easily be a plus factor in one part of a city and a minus factor in another. This is true also of the property types: In the same community, residences in the $18,500 class may have remained stable, residences in the $8,500 class may have dropped to $7,500, industrial land may have increased in value approximately 25%, while commercial lots have enhanced 150%, all within the same period. There is, therefore, no shortcut for applying this adjustment; it must be recomputed for *each property appraised and each comparable sale* used in each appraisal.

The adjustment for time of sale is often simply added in with the other sales adjustments. This is incorrect procedure when percentage adjustments are applied. The time adjustment must be completed, and an adjusted indication of value derived before application of any of the other percentage sale adjustments. The prior completion of this adjustment is necessary because the other (subsequent) adjustments apply to the *present* comparable property. For example, if the comparable sale price is $3 per square foot and adjustment for time of sale is 15%, and subject location is rated 10% better than that of the comparable property, then the adjustment for location is 10% of $3.45, not of $3.

Elements of Time Adjustment—The adjustment for time of sale is often made by the formation of only one judgment, as is indicated in the frequent use of "X% per year." In an improved property, however, three major factors are reflected by this one estimate, and the separate analysis of each of these factors will reduce the probable range of error involved in the single judgment method. These elements are as follows:

1. Construction cost new (usually has increased).
2. Condition and functional utility of improvements (usually had declined).
3. Land value (usually has increased).

Other sub-elements may be considered to affect the time of sale adjustment, such as special market conditions for the locality, or for the property type, but any other factors would ultimately be of significance only insofar as they raised or lowered one of the foregoing three elements.

Location—This adjustment has to do, not with the site as does the accessibility location, but with the *relation* of the site to other sites and improvements, nearness and direction of the growth of the type of development contemplated in the estimate of highest and best use, or of related uses.

The adjustment for location is not to be confused with that for lot value. In considering the sale of a residence or other improved property, the adjustment to be accounted for by this factor is quite often considerably more than would be accounted for by the differences in lot value of the two properties. For example, in one local neighborhood, a differential for location was found between houses on two streets amounting to a $1,500 price differential, while only a $500 differential was indicated for difference in lot values.

Size-Improvements—In an adjustment on an improved comparable sale property, confusion sometimes results when adjustments are made for some factor involving area of the subject property. This confusion can be avoided by the following rule: "Minus" adjustments (subject inferior to comparable) are factors of the comparable property area; "plus" adjustments (subject superior to comparable) are factors of the subject property area. This rule would apply to any item which was a factor of size, such as construction, air conditioning, basement, heating, etc.

When adjusting for size of improvement, it should be borne in mind that, generally speaking, excess area of subject over that of the comparable building is not as costly as the base rate applicable to the comparable building. For example, if a 5,000 sq. ft. comparable sale building cost $10 per sq. ft., and subject is a 7,000 sq. ft. building, then subject's cost of the 2,000 sq. ft. difference (and adjustment to the sale price therefor) will normally be a rate somewhat less than $10 per square foot.

After the Adjusted Indication—After the derivation of an adjusted indication of value, the series of adjusted indications may at first glance appear to leave the appraiser no closer to the value than he was at the point of unadjusted sale prices. It is therefore helpful sometimes to rearrange these adjusted indications so that they form a more meaningful pattern. Four methods of doing this may be mentioned:

1. *By Array:* This means, simply, lining up the adjusted indications of value in ascending or descending order. Quite often, after doing so, the appraiser will easily see that one or two somewhat high adjusted indications and one or two somewhat low indications may have left the result with an appearance of confusion, whereas merely lining them up in order will reveal a definite pattern.

2. *By Most Important Physical Characteristic:* In each case, the most important physical characteristic may vary. For example, when the subject property is a larger tract than most of the comparable sale properties, the extraction of only the larger comparable sales may show a pattern of adjusted indications of value from these particular sales, different from that indicated by the sales less physically comparable.

3. *By Adjusted Indication With the Smallest Net Adjustment:* For example, extraction of the adjusted indications which have no more than, say, 10% or 15% plus or minus net adjustments, will often reveal justification of separate consideration for these particular sales indications.

4. *By Most Recent Sales:* Extraction and separate consideration of the most recent sales in the group (say, those with either no adjustment or small adjustment for time of

sale) often reduce the apparent spread of adjusted indications and shed more light on the indicated value.

The adjusted value indications, thus separated for analysis of the particular points which the appraiser may feel more important in the specific appraisal, may be considered further by selection of the mean, median, and mode from any or all of the resulting groups of indications.

Weighting—A final analysis of each adjusted indication of value may be effected by assigning a proportionate weight to each adjusted value indication, giving each its share of the final value estimate. For example, with four adjusted indications, each of exactly equal validity to the other, and given the same weight in the final value estimate, each adjusted indication obviously is accorded, consciously or unconsciously, a weight of 25% of the final value estimate.

If, however, one sale of the four is considerably more recent than the others, nearer to subject, then it may be that the appraiser will prefer to assign a weight of 40% to one sale and weight of 20% to each of the other three sales. This procedure is often a useful tool in the drawing of final conclusions from the adjusted sale indications.

Magnitude of Adjustment—In accordance with the premise that no adjustment is better than any adjustment, it necessarily follows that, generally speaking, a small adjustment is better than a large adjustment. This, however, is not in all cases true.

It is not necessarily the size, either in absolute terms or in proportionate terms, of the adjustment which determines its degree of validity; this is determined by the degree to which the particular adjustment may be substantiated by the market. For example, a house with extra land in a neighborhood with plentiful sales of comparable lots, may require a $10,000 adjustment for lot value, which, however, is quite supportable, so that the comparable property is easily usable in valuation of subject, while a $500 or $750 adjustment for time of sale or for architectural style may be considerably more conjectural.

The Difference Method:

For an illustration of the importance of differences only, one needs only to recall that the minimum F.H.A. specifications for a "basic house" requires two full typewritten pages, with separate description of excavation, foundations, exterior walls, gables, floor framing, subflooring, finish flooring, partition framing, etc.

When rating a comparable against a subject, though, rather than requiring a 2-page, or even a lengthy paragraph of description of construction for the comparable, our problem may be stated simply as: What is the difference between these two houses? If we assume that House A is a comparable sale property, and House B is a subject property, then we could quite easily find ourselves forgetting the real problem in wading through a mass of description. The significant differences between the subject and the comparable can usually be expressed in one line: "No fireplace in A," "No air conditioning in B," "Half basement and extra bath in B," etc. This is the *difference,* and this is all that is of any relevance in comparing one property with another and deriving therefrom an indication of market value.

A considerable amount of completely wasted time, energy, and money is expended in appraisal reports, whether in individual narrative formats, or in forms supplied by governmental agencies, or companies which have forms for company transfer appraisals. Time is wasted in listing either lengthy physical descriptions of comparable properties or in neighborhood data called for in many appraisal forms.

What does it matter, for instance, in a residential appraisal, where the schools are, where the churches are, what the commuter fare is, where the buslines are, what the distance to shopping is, etc.? The answer is simply that it does not matter at all. In a single family residential appraisal, the value estimate is normally derived completely from the comparable sale data by accounting for the variances or differences between the sale properties and the subject property.

The sale properties are, in most residential appraisals, within a block or two of the subject property, and similar in locational factors. If the subject is two miles from a shopping center, it is a reasonably safe bet that the comparable properties used will also be approximately two miles from the same shopping center, since the comparable sales are taken from the same immediate area as the subject property and are subject to the same neighborhood, community, and regional factors as is the subject property.

If it were stated in the report that only the differences are being considered, the subject property could be described with much less detail, and no description whatever of the comparable properties need be given, excepting *only* the *differences* between comparable and subject (such as "no fireplace," "no air conditioning," etc.).

Delimiting the Range of Value:

A basic step in the translation of market data into value indicators is the delimitation of the range of value; that is, the establishment of upper and lower limits at which points a purchase would be uneconomic for the purchaser or a sale would be uneconomic for a seller. Upon establishment of these two points, the appraiser may then begin to narrow this range.

With a simple refinement to this technique, the appraiser can get much closer to the final value indication than is generally realized. Along with a systematic realignment of the data, we use the single judgment factors of "superior" and "inferior," from which a reasonably narrower range is derived.

Combining this single judgment for each comparable, with the extraction of the highest "low" indication and the lowest "high" indication, delimits the indicated value range more closely than is often the case with an elaborate grid type of adjustment chart. This method of comparison of market data may be seen in Figure 8.1, taken from a page of an appraisal report on an old industrial property. The abbreviations are S for superior, I for inferior, E for equivalent.

This type of "single judgment" comparison, when combined with an *orderly realignment* of the sales prices, leads much more easily and in a more explicable manner, to a value indication which lies within a closer range than that usually resulting from a series of adjustments to the sale prices. In this example, the indicated value range of the original sale prices, from $3.07 to $5.06 per square foot, was narrowed to a range of $3.75 to $4.55.

Market Data Summary

Sale #	Price Per Sq. Ft.	Construction Age, and Condition	Functional Utility	Land Coverage	Site	Location	Overall Comparison Rating
1.	$3.18	S	S	S	I	I	I
2.	4.55	S	E	I	E	S	S
3.	3.07	S	E	I	E	I	I
4.	3.22	E	E	I	E	E	I
5.	4.46	S	E	I	I	E	E
6.	5.06	E	E	I	S	S	S
7.	3.75	E	I	S	E	I	I

Although the prices of the comparable sale properties ranged from $3.07 to $5.06 per sq. ft., it may easily be seen that the range of value indication is considerably narrowed by realigning the sale data as in Figure 8.1.

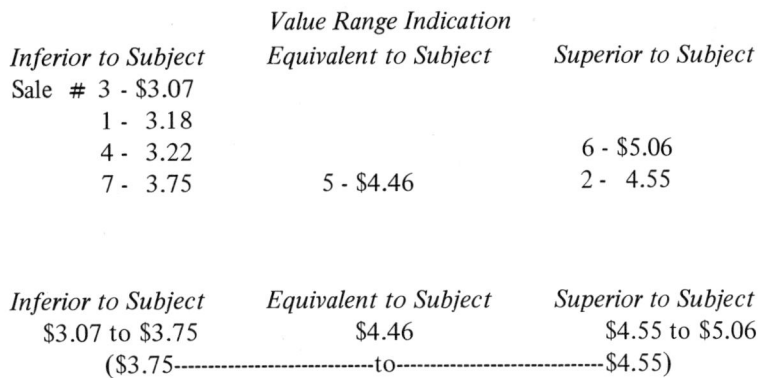

Value Range Indication

Inferior to Subject	*Equivalent to Subject*	*Superior to Subject*
Sale # 3 - $3.07		
1 - 3.18		
4 - 3.22		6 - $5.06
7 - 3.75	5 - $4.46	2 - 4.55

Inferior to Subject	*Equivalent to Subject*	*Superior to Subject*
$3.07 to $3.75	$4.46	$4.55 to $5.06

($3.75----------------------------to----------------------------$4.55)

Figure 8.1
Value Range Indication

I submit that this method of delimiting the range of value, supplemented, when appropriate, by one adjustment only, that for "time of sale," so that the prices used are the prices adjusted for time of sale only, results in a much more logical and supportable value indication than that resulting from a sequence of adjustments applied to each comparable property.

The Base Property Technique:

Suppose you are making a rental appraisal, and have gathered and analyzed comparable rental data for one of your subject units, shown in Figure 8.2.

Building # T-XX
Family Housing (1 story, detached single family residence)

Comparable rental houses may be adjusted to similarity with Subject as follows:

Comp. #	Rent	Constr. & Condition	Size & Utility	Kitchen, Bth., Htg.	Car Storage
8	$90				+$5.00
9	85	-$2.50	-$5.00	+$5.00	
14	80	- 2.50	- 2.50	+ 2.50	
15	70	+ 7.50	- 1.00		
18	75	- 3.50			+ 5.00

(Continued)

Comp. #	Site & Location	Furn. and Furnishings	Equip.	Adjusted Indication Basic Shelter Rent
8	+$2.50	-$12.50	-$5.00	$80.00
9	+ 2.50	- 12.50		72.50
14	+ 2.50			80.00
15	+ 3.50			80.00
18	+ 5.00			81.50

Best Comparables: #8, #15, #18

Indicated Basic Shelter Rent
(mo.) $80.00

Figure 8.2
Rental Housing Adjustments

To arrive at the indicated basic shelter rent per month, $80, 35 individual judgments have been made. Now, you are ready to price the second building in your subject project. Using the conventional adjustment chart, as illustrated above, five comparable properties are analyzed with respect to seven different property features (or independent variables).

The base property technique may be applied to analysis of the second and/or subsequent similar properties, shown in Figure 8.3.

Building #T-XX
Base property is taken as Building #T-XX, at basic shelter rent of:	$80.00
Adjusted upward for Construction and Condition	+2.50
Adjusted downward for Car Storage	-5.00
And downward for Site and Location	-2.50
Indicated basic shelter rent =	$75.00

Figure 8.3
Base Property Technique

The use of the preceding appraised property as a base property results in the need for only *3* adjustments rather than *35*. It also results in the client's having to explain only a *$5* rent differential, rather than the whole *$75*, and permits him to compare this property with another *subject* property in explaining this rental, rather than going back to each of the comparable properties and attempting to explain each of the adjustments applied to the comparables.

Just as 3 adjustments are easier to explain than 35, by the same token, a $5 figure is easier to explain than a $75 figure. At the present time, at least two governmental agencies permit this technique.

There is no reason why it should not be used on any type of mass appraisal assignment, for instance, on highway takings, or urban renewal acquisitions, where numerous fairly similar properties in a row are acquired.

Conclusions:

In adjusting or correlating sales, rentals, costs, or other market data to produce a final value estimate, the appraiser must remain aware that the comparable data used represent past history. They may be thought of as a sequence of "still shots," snapped in the midst of the constant flux of a highly imperfect market. The estimate of present value should always be placed within its context of the direction and velocity of the forces of supply and effective demand. The appraiser's reasoning must, as nearly as possible, simulate that of the persons creating the market.

The viewpoint of the seller and the buyer are the appraiser's only ultimate recourse in the valuing process. There are no "intrinsic" or "inherent" property values to assist him in his problem, for value, like beauty, lies not in that beheld, but in the eye of the beholder.

IX

How Replacement Costs Are Used
in the Substitution Process

As is commonly known in the profession, the "cost approach" to value is almost never used in the actual value estimate, except in case of special purpose properties, otherwise being merely added to the appraisal after the value conclusion has been reached. In the case of existing residential properties, when there is any appreciable amount of market activity, the cost approach is not used in actually estimating value.

Fallacies of Cost Approach:

The cost approach rationale necessarily assumes that the sum of the parts (land, site improvements, building, less various sorts of depreciation) is equal to the whole. Since the various factors do not contribute separately to the property value, but interact upon each other, this assumption cannot be correct except by chance.

This "approach," moreover, assumes a land value as if vacant and available for a higher use, while assigning value to the improvement as is. This assumption of two disparate but simultaneous uses for portions of the property is in obvious conflict with elementary logic.

The approach also, by definition, assumes the equivalence of cost and value for the "as new" property. This beginning point of the approach thus starts on an untenable premise.

The use of the cost approach was initiated during the depression years, when property sales were scarce, and such as occurred did not fit the appraiser's preconception of "normal" value. This reasoning is unjustifiable however, when ample market data are available. It is now recognized that there is no more a "normal" value than there is a "normal" year; the term is meaningless in view of the appraiser's function, which is to predict what a seller and purchaser would most likely do now.

Time Factor in Replacement:

A cost new estimate may be invalidated by the time element in replacement. The appraiser should always be certain that he is dealing with actual alternatives available to the owner or purchaser rather than hypothetical buildings: if relocation would require 18 months, and 18 months would eliminate a property from operation, then the time element obviates practicability of replacement, and replacement is therefore not a usable alternative in the valuation.

Uses of Replacement Cost:

Why then, a chapter devoted to replacement cost? Because this is a tool usable by the appraiser, in pricing alternatives available to the purchaser, estimating cost to cure certain deficiencies, determining feasibility of given improvement programs, and estimating warranted cost for an entrepreneur or investor.

Reproduction and Replacement:

Since estimation of reproduction costs of existing improvements is still espoused by segments of the appraisal establishment, the subject will be touched upon here only to remind the reader that reproduction cost is in all such cases irrelevant to his problem of market value. No time should be wasted on a circular exercise of estimating cost of improvements which would in no circumstances be reproduced. The only cost relevant is that of replacement of the improvement's utility and function with such a structure as would serve the function and which would in fact be built if the existing improvements were gone.

In this regard, reproduction cost is not always necessarily higher than replacement cost, as is often assumed. An example is a food processing plant of cheap construction with concrete slab floors, painted block interior finish, and normal squared corners. While such a structure may continue its present use, it could not be reproduced, but instead would be replaced with more expensive construction fitting the USDA's requirements, with tile floors, glazed tile walls, more expensive doors, and rounded corners.

Derivation of Cost Estimates:

While published cost services are usable for occasional rough checks on building costs, they are far inferior in local validity to a good file of actual specific building costs in the appraiser's territory.

Contractor's cost estimates are usually less reliable than the actual building costs accumulated by the typical appraiser over a period of a few years. Familiarity with the range between high and low bids submitted by contractors, running 10%, 20%, and 30% indicates that the appraiser should not feel so diffident before a contractor's cost estimate, particularly as these estimates typically vary much more than the range expected in the appraiser's final value estimate. The contractor's estimate deals with a hypothetical building, while completed contract costs reflect an existing cost base which may be adjusted to comparability with the subject building.

The most reliable replacement cost for residences is obtained as follows:

1. Select a number of recent sales of new houses in the various classes of construction.
2. Establish typical lot values by sales in these or similar neighborhoods.
3. Subtract lot value and site improvement cost from the sale price. The remainder is the most accurate and pertinent building cost available—the final cost to the ultimate purchaser. This may most easily be reduced to a square foot cost by percentaging the extra construction items such as porches and carports. The resulting total effective square footage yields the cost per square foot of livable area.

Construction of a Comparable:

The principal use for replacement cost, aside from determination of proposed investment return, is in constructing a new "comparable" for the subject property. The result is as valid a comparable as is derived from sale data, when the constructed comparable is one of the substitutes or actual alternatives available to the owner or purchaser. If such a hypothetical structure would not in fact be built in the current market, or if the delay in building it would put the occupant out of business, or if no reasonably located site is available, then such alternative is not available to subject, and does not represent a substitute in value for the subject property.

Replacement of Site:

In "constructing" such a substitute building, clearly, the building would not be placed on the subject site, but on the substitute site, so the land value of the substitute site is the proper land value to use in this approach. Although this point was emphasized by Bonbright[1] in 1937, it has been improperly ignored with a considerable degree of consistency.

---

[1] James C. Bonbright, *Valuation of Property,* Volume I (Charlottesville, Va.: The Michie Co., 1937), p. 153. Copyright 1937, by James C. Bonbright.

In estimating a replacement for a multi-story light industrial building in a near-downtown area, for instance, the substitute building would most likely be a one story building and would likely be located on a site considerably larger than subject site, but priced at less per square foot. The vital point is to use only available and feasible alternatives.

After estimating cost new of a replacement property, the resultant property should be treated as a comparable sale, with adjustments applied for comparability with subject.

In appraising a special purpose property such as a church, for example, the replacement site would have to be one that the particular congregation would actually use; church site sales on the opposite side of town would be completely irrelevant. If acceptable sites are completely built up with residences, then the substitute property should simply contemplate the purchase of dwelling site and demolition for the church construction.

Capital Improvement Feasibility:

The feasibility of proposed capital improvements to a property may be exemplified as follows: Subject is an eight unit apartment house, with proposed improvements consisting of gas furnace conversion, asphalt tile floor cover, kitchen cabinets, ranges, and wall ovens. The increase in rent obtainable after the improvements is $2,000. Increase in expenses by virtue of improvements is $200.

$$\begin{array}{r} \$2,000 \\ - \ 200 \\ \hline \$1,800 \end{array}$$

Cost of the improvements total $12,000. Return on the $12,000 investment is 15%. Since the overall property return is placed at 10%, initiation of the improvement program is advisable as a profitable investment.

Entrepreneur's Warranted Cost:

Occasionally the consultant is presented a problem as to warranted cost, somewhat as follows: An entrepreneur is tentatively interested in purchasing a particular site, and constructing a particular type of improvement, say an auto service center, with an approximate rental established. He needs not only an appraisal of the proposed property, but the warranted amount he can invest in the building, and the size of the building. This may be computed as follows:

1. Lot cost	$20,000
2. Approximate rent $450/mo.	$ 5,400
3. Proposed property value (land and building package)	
Rent ....$ 5,400
Less vacancy and expense total ....$ 1,350

Net rental . . . .$ 4,050
At 9% equals value of $45,000
4. Entrepreneur's acceptable profit 20%:
  $45,000/120%-$37,500 warranted total cost,
5. Warranted total cost is $37,500
Less lot price $20,000
Warranted building cost $17,500
at $7 per square foot, equals building
size obtainable of 2,500 square feet.
If the proposed tenant finds this size and
type of building acceptable, the project
is feasible. The property upon completion
will be saleable to an investor at
$45,000, with lump sum profit to the
developer of $7,500.

X

How and When
Accrued Depreciation Is
Measured

The estimate of accrued depreciation is properly used only in the function of adjustment factors to a substitute property which could and most likely would be actually constructed as an alternative choice to the subject property. Regardless of the format in which a depreciation estimate is applied, the estimate is in effect merely a breakdown of the effective age estimate, which must by definition include all depreciating factors.

Rent Loss Capitalization:

Some of the flaws inherent in the basic assumptions of the rent loss method of depreciation estimation are as follows:

1. The ascending scale of rent does not follow the same curve of increment as that of prices, neither for the same properties, nor the same class of property, nor for all properties in total.

2. Increasing rents hit plateaus and eventual stopping points. Prices for the same properties level off, but never completely so, as do rents.

3. The relation of a rent differential is not necessarily in the same ratio to a price of the property as was the basic rent of the property. The differential, or the rent loss

being capitalized, whether "gross" or "net," may be just the difference between profit and loss. This reasoning applies to gross rent exactly the same as it does to net rent, since net is a function of gross.

As an illustration of this, the following is a specific example of sales of two houses, directly across the street from each other. One sold for $8,000, and was rented at $60; the other sold for $12,000 and was rented at $65. Question: What is the monthly multiple for the rent differential between the two houses? (Both prices and both rentals in this example were valid.) The multiple for the $8,000 house is 133; the multiple for the $12,000 house is 185. Before you choose either of these figures, however, consider this: the price differential of $4,000 divided by the rent differential of $5 indicates a multiple of 800. The explanation for the existence of these three multiples, completely unamenable to meaningful relation to the comparable properties, is simple: the rent "topped out" and the price did not.

4. This method assumes that each dollar of gross rent contributes the same amount of value; that is, that gross and net are interchangeable. This conclusion, of necessity, follows the assumption that the multiple for the total property is the correct multiple to apply to a rent loss differential representing a fractional part of the property.

5. Multipliers are derived only by dividing an adjusted sale price of a comparable property by its rents, so that, for residential property, the entire operation starts with the answer: that is, a multiple is derived from a sale adjusted to subject, which sale therefore reflects the dollar amount of this obsolescence item and also already reflects the value of the subject property.

6. Alternatively, the rent loss figures for estimates both of incurable obsolescence and of economic obsolescence are estimates of rental loss from an estimated rental obtainable for an assumed ideal property, or one not having the particular deficiency contributing to this form of obsolescence. The multiple used is an estimate of what the multiple would be for this property if it were rented and if it were either affected or unaffected by the particular depreciating factor.

The result of multiplying an estimate by another estimate is of highly questionable validity.

7. Since rents and reductions of rent affect an entire property, the market does not supply sufficiently fragmented data for an appraiser to make supportable estimates of rent loss attributable to all of the various components and functions of a property.

In a typical text demonstration of the rent loss method of depreciation estimation, it is determined that the gross annual multiple for the class of property including subject is 5. It is also concluded that the total economic rent is $8,000. A rent loss estimate of $1,000 is made and multiplied by the gross annual multiple of 5 to give an indication of $5,000 in depreciation.

Aside from the fact that the answer to the valuation problem (5 x 8,000 = $40,000 value) is obtained *before* the depreciation estimate is made, the following illustrates the fallacy of this method:

If the rental is $1,000 less than it would be without the depreciating factor, the

Gross potential rent		$8,000
Less vacancy allowance (5%)		800
Effective Gross Rental		$7,200

Expenses:

Taxes	$1,000	
Insurance	440	
Repairs & Maintenance	800	
Management	360	
Jan., misc.	600	$3,200
	NET RENTAL	$4,000
	@ 10% = $40,000 value	

Change attributable to the depreciating item, @ 5 x gross rent loss. $5,000

Deducting depreciating item from rent:

Effective rental	$7,200
Deducting rent loss	1,000
Adjusted Effective Gross Rental	$6,200

Expenses:

Taxes	$1,000	
Insurance	440	
Repairs & Maintenance	800	
Management	310	
Jan., misc.	600	3,150
	NET RENTAL	$3,050
	@ 10% = $30,500 value	

Actual depreciation from the $1,000 loss therefore is:	$40,000
	30,500
Actual depr. from $1,000 rent loss	$ 9,500

appraiser should simply deduct this amount from his gross rental estimate, and complete his income calculation accordingly. He would see, of course, that, assuming typical expense ratios, his multiplier technique for estimating obsolescence greatly misstates the depreciation.

The only expense reduced in proportion to gross rental deduction would be the managment expense. Thus, the gross income loss represents approximately a 90% net income loss. Carrying the rent loss estimate through to its logical conclusion would result somewhat as is shown above.

Thus, it may easily be seen that the actual depreciation in the given example would be underestimated by $4,500.

If it is assumed in the valuation that taxes may be reduced in the same proportion as the rent reduction from gross potential rental (12.5%), expense for taxes would be $875, making a total expense figure of $3,025 and net rental of $3,175, resulting in a value of $31,750.

Deducting from the value indicated for the "without depreciation" property: $40,000 minus $31,750 = $8,250 depreciation rather than $5,000, indicating understatement of depreciation of $3,250.

The Breakdown Method:

The standard "breakdown method" of depreciation estimation, in breaking down the various depreciating factors into the conventional five classes of depreciation, establishes inconsistent mathematical ratios between these various elements, which are so interlocking that not even the most proficient exponents of this method have been able to maintain these ratios consistently from start to finish of a demonstration of accrued depreciation.

Since the mathematical fallacies of the break-down method have been examined in detail elsewhere,[1] only the estimate of Physical Incurable Depreciation will be discussed briefly here. A typical text example is as follows:

Total reproduction cost new is $142,000. Remaining economic life is estimated at 40 years, or 85% of 47 years total economic life. Effective age, therefore, is estimated at 7 years, or 15% of total economic life. This 7/47, or 15%, is taken as Physical Incurable Depreciation, amounting to $21,300. All depreciation is subsequently totalled to $37,080.

If effective age, however, is properly defined as Expired economic life/Total economic life, then the estimate of $21,300, representing the effective age, *is* total accrued depreciation, from whatever cause. This unnecessary, circular, "whole as a part of the whole" calculation has been institutionalized in the profession since about 1940. Since it of necessity arrives at an answer which must be determined *prior* to the calculation, I urge that it be dispensed with, and that the time be more profitably employed in more thoroughly analyzing the market.

Under-Improvement:

An under-improvement is often cited as suffering from depreciation, usually classified as functional obsolescence. No text examined, however, explains how the building value is reduced by virtue of being an under-improvement of the land. A typical example cited is a $10,000 house in a $20,000 neighborhood. In actual practice, it would appear that the $10,000 house would be slightly enhanced by its more expensive surroundings, if all depreciation or appreciation is considered to apply to improvements, which is the assumption of all texts examined. If the total value new (land and improvements), however, is considered to be of reduced value, then it must be conceded that the land has been depreciated, which, in fact, is the case.

[1] Gene Dilmore, "The Estimate of Accrued Depreciation," *The Real Estate Appraiser*, June 1965.

Economic Life:

There is no such thing as a predictable 40 or 50 year "life" for a building. Both expensive structures razed after 12 or 15 years and 600 and 700 year old buildings in Europe should dispel this fallacy by their very existence.

Bone Structure:

The bone structure theory is used in the "breakdown method" of depreciation estimation, in the estimate of incurable physical deterioration. Since this estimate requires a figure for total accrued depreciation for its calculation as a percentage thereof, it would appear that the bone structure process is entirely redundant, since the appraiser has the answer before he does this calculation.

It appears highly questionable that there is such a phenomenon as is designated by the term "incurable physical deterioration," since physical deterioration is always a result of some form of obsolescence. Physical deterioration occurs subsequent to, and because of, functional or economic factors which caused some person to *allow* physical deterioration.

The bone structure calculation is not a direct estimation of physical depreciation, but a method of testing a previously made depreciation estimate. This is true also of fractional calculations of other incurable items of depreciation, since the ultimate function of these computations is to test the effective age estimate.

For classes of property generally sold rather than rented, price differentials attributable to functional and economic obsolescence factors are much easier to find and support in the market than are rent losses attributable thereto.

Rent loss capitalization is inappropriate for the estimation of accrued depreciation in residential appraisals, and should be discarded from demonstrations and texts illustrating techniques of residential appraising. In the case of income properties, if the appraiser estimates a loss in rent of a given amount, it would be simpler and more accurate for him to deduct the rent loss from the economic rent of the property, and proceed with the balance of his income approach, as it is the change in net income which is of vital importance.

Despite the artificial division of "three approaches," with their concomitant subdivisions, only one value is sought. After it is found, the employment of scientific appearing but mathematically unsound techniques of measuring depreciation, to reduce "cost new" to the value found, lengthens appraisal reports, but does not enhance the veridity of the value estimate.

Obsolescence—Church:

In the valuation of a church, where no sales for a continuation of the same use are available in the area, replacement cost new less depreciation is the only available means of valuation. The most difficult part of the depreciation estimate in this case is economic obsolescence. An imperfect but quite helpful measure of economic obsolescence may be derived as follows: The subject neighborhood may be designated as consisting of the census tract or tracts in which the subject's congregation lives. The change over a period of time in median family income in these census tracts may be analyzed by pairing the change in the subject tracts, and in the total city. If the subject tract shows a relatively lower increase, a reduction in value is indicated. This percentage, of course, does not necessarily coincide precisely with the true economic obsolescence, but furnishes a definite guide to the general level of obsolescence accruing.

Depreciation—Service Station:

A frequently occurring problem is the estimate of effective age for a service station. Each case warrants close study, as obsolescence of this type of property appears to be accelerating constantly. A guide to economic life is consideration of the prevalent lease terms; the base period is the only period safely projected for life of improvements, as this is all that the oil companies are definitely counting on.

Further guidance may be found by examining the records of demolitions; assessment records show the age of these specific structures at time of demolition.

The principle use of the concept of depreciation is not altered from that stated by Bonbright (James C. Bonbright, *Valuation of Property*, Vol. 1, p. 214) in 1937: for the deduction of value inferiorities from an actually available alternative. And this is done only with an alternative which is available; that is, improvements which would actually be constructed on an alternative and available site are penalized for the value inferiorities indicated in comparison of the subject property with the alternative property.

XI

Methods of Income
Capitalization

$\mathbf{T}$here are three basic methods of capitalization in use:

1. *Straight Line.* This method simply uses income divided by interest or return rate. Straight line capitalization is sometimes classified as an annuity with income decline of a specific type (interest x recapture/interest + recapture). In view of its widespread use, however, as an expression of the ratio of income to value, or earnings to price, it may be considered as a separate method.

While income divided by price is a valid measure of a relationship between these two elements, the capitalization of income by the straight line method as actually applied by practicing appraisers in the residual techniques assumes a level income, level recapture, and level interest. These three assumptions are not arithmetically compatible, being a direct contradiction in terms. (The author has never encountered an appraiser who actually calculated the income decline of $\frac{i \times r}{i + r}$ in a real appraisal.)

It is improper, moreover, to adjust the return rate in order to reflect a purported assumption with respect to the level of income. The income projection should be adjusted to reflect any such assumption.

2. *Sinking Fund Method.* This method of capitalization assumes level income, and

return of capital in one lump sum at the end of the economic life of the improvement. The recapture money is discounted at a "safe" interest rate for its accumulation to total improvement value at the end of the improvement life. This method will tend to understate the recapture of capital, unless a sinking fund is in fact established for the property.

If such a fund is not in fact established, the appraiser has no logical basis on which to apply any second rate to reinvestment of recapture.

3. *Annuity Method:* This method may assume either a level, declining, increasing or fluctuating income, with recapture being the remainder of total return less that portion attributable to the property interest rate on the remaining balance. This method is adaptable to changing income patterns by merely altering the income discounted for particular years. This is the most mathematically sound method of capitalization.

Return of Improvements Over a "Period of Economic Life": The widely used method of capitalization by the residual techniques contemplates the return of the investment in improvements, over the "life of the building." Recapture of the capital investment, however, as actually provided for by an investor in making his purchase, does not necessarily equate with the usual concept of depreciation in the sense of wearing out of the building. The recapture period is the period over which the investor gets his money back. Recapture of the invested capital, in actuality, is generally accomplished by resale of the property.

If properties were in reality held in one ownership for the economic lives of the buildings, which is the implied assumption of the traditional residual techniques, our market data would consist entirely of properties with newly completed improvements or with totally depreciated improvements, that is, land sales.

Improper Use of the Residual Techniques as an Intended Reflection of Market Behavior: Sales in the market rarely involve a capitalization rate composed of an interest rate for land and buildings, plus a recapture rate for the annual portion of the economic life of the building, as is assumed in the land residual and building residual techniques. The following is a typical employment of a capitalization rate derived from the market and applied by the building residual technique:

Sale price of comparable property, $100,000; net income, $8,000; overall rate, 8%; land value for subject estimated at $40,000; economic life estimated for subject, 40 years. The 8% rate derived from the sale is usually employed approximately as follows:

Net rental of subject	$8,000
Land value $40,000 at 8%	3,200
Attributable to improvements	$4,800

Capitalized at 8% interest plus 2.5% recapture equals:

Improvements	$45,700
plus Land value	40,000
TOTAL VALUE INDICATION	$85,700

Assuming, thus, that subject property is equivalent to the comparable property, value of subject by this method is understated by $14,300. If this sale were to be used, the residual technique would require the following method:

Overall rate		.080
Improvements .60 x Recapture .025 =		.015
	Interest Rate	.065

Applied to Subject:

Net rental	$8,000
Land value $40,000 @ 6.5%	2,600
Attributable to improvements	$5,400

Capitalized at 6.5% interest plus 2.5% recapture
        equals:

	Improvements	$ 60,000
plus	Land	40,000
	TOTAL VALUE	$100,000

It is submitted that the market does not break down investments in existing properties in this manner. The two crucial factors of remaining economic life and land/improvements ratio are subject to violent manipulation, depending on the "judgment" of the appraiser, and depending on the interest rate he desires to extract.

The Concept of Perpetuity: In view of the obvious impossibility of predicting an income stream, and therefore, economic life, for the life of an improvement, the fallacy of predicting a perpetual income or perpetual value is equally obvious.

This concept, moreover, is not pertinent to the appraiser's problem, as may be seen in a tabulation of the present worth of 1 per year at, say, an 8% return rate, at intervals of 10 years:

Years	Factors
10	6.71
20	9.82
30	11.26
40	11.92
50	12.23
60	12.38
70	12.44
80	12.47
90	12.49
100	12.49
Perpetuity	12.50

In this way, we can easily see that, at this rate of return, the first ten years of a $10,000 per year income would be worth $67,100 while the balance of the income stream, extending into the future for all eternity, would be worth only $57,900. At a 10% rate, the disparity is even greater, the first 10 years of income being worth $61.450, and the balance to perpetuity being worth only $38,550.

Consequently, the first few years of income are so important, in conversion to present worth, that very long term or perpetual income simply is not a necessary concept for valuation.

How Income is Capitalized: The eristic straight line methods and residual techniques do not give a return rate in terms consistent with measures of return on alternative investments.

It is undisputed, however, that money accumulates forward in time by one method only, in the pattern of $(1 + i)^n$. Since this is the pattern of forward accumulation, it should be equally clear that future incomes discount to their present worth in the reciprocal of the same pattern, $\frac{1}{(1 + i)^n}$. This we recognize as the familiar reversion factor. With this simple factor, any pattern of incomes may be reduced to present worth.

Since all interest accumulates in the same way, $(1 + i)^n$, it follows that all differences in capitalization methods consist entirely of differences in recapture assumptions.

Traditional appraisal theory attributes these recapture differences to variations in assumptions regarding reinvestment of the recaptured funds. For example, it is stated that the Hoskold, or sinking fund method, assumes reinvestment at the safe rate, while the Inwood, or annuity method, assumes reinvestment at the property risk rate.

If, however, one applies to the problem the venerable principle of Ockham's Razor, it may be seen that use of a capitalization method requires no assumption whatever with respect to reinvestment of recaptured funds. This results from the definition of recapture, which I propose to state as: Recapture = Return - Interest. That is, recapture may be conceived of as simply the arithmetic difference between the total return earned, and that part of the return representing the interest on the outstanding investment.

A usage analogous to this concept of no reinvestment assumption may be noted in the Ellwood Process, in which that part of the capitalization rate representing expected value decline is discounted by the sinking fund factor without assuming actual establishment of a sinking fund. Moreover, recaptured funds may be reinvested at any rate obtainable at time of recapture, which would coincide only by chance with the currently estimated property rate of return.

Recaptured funds of most industrial and business firms are generally, in fact, reinvested at the firm's earnings rate, with respect to which its real estate investment may be a minor factor. Recaptured funds, for that matter, may not be reinvested at all, but spent. The rate at which they are reinvested, if reinvested, is therefore not amenable to estimation. In view of the frequent impossibility of making this purported reinvestment assumption, it is fortunate that there is no necessity to do so.

For practical application of these concepts, further definitions are in order:

Equity: the present worth of all expected incomes.

Incomes: All spendable cash flows, regardless of source.

Capitalization: discounting to present worth of each cash flow by the reversion factor for its internal rate of return. If the net income to be capitalized is level, then this is shortened by applying the annuity, or Inwood factor.

Internal rate of return: that rate at which the sum of the discounted cash flows, including reversion of the terminal value, equals the initial investment.

It is calculated as follows: Find the rate at which: $\Sigma \frac{1}{(1+i)} \cdot$ 1st yr spendable cash $+ \frac{1}{(1+i)^2} \cdot$ 2nd yr spendable cash. $\ldots \cdot \frac{1}{(1+i)^n} \cdot$ nth yr spendable cash $+ \frac{1}{(1+i)^n} \cdot$ nth yr after tax cash reversion = beginning investment.

Since total value always equals mortgage plus equity, the basic valuation equation may be reduced to $E = \Sigma$ (IR); that is, Equity equals the sum of (Incomes x Reversion factors). (Note that the equity may be more or less than the initial investment.)

It is evident that a cash flow is not actually spendable income to the investor until the income tax thereon has been accounted for. It is therefore suggested that spendable cash flows and after-tax reversions be projected somewhat along the lines of the accompanying example. (Figure 11.1 A, B, C and D). This format is only partly original, and owes something to both Dr. James Graaskamp's Compraisal format, and to that proposed by M. B. Hodges, Jr. in "Ellwood Plus," *The Real Estate Appraiser,* Sept., 1969. It may be expanded, of course, to embrace further refinements, such as accounting for conjunctive personal property depreciation, state income taxes, etc. The particular format is predicated on the idea that the internal rate of return is the one most meaningful rate, and is constructed principally for derivation of this one figure.

The format is also adaptable to computer use, whereby the appraiser may be relieved of the numerous repetitive computations. On Line 37, only the results of the present worth/rate calculations are given.

The example, taken from one of the author's recent appraisals, is a proposed $650,000 property, with land value of $72,500, and improvements of $577,500. Financing was obtainable on a 70% loan ratio, at 9.5% interest rate, for a 20 year term. The investor has a 50% marginal tax rate.

On the Return Analysis section Lines 1 through 23 do not assume resale; from Line 24 on, resale is assumed for *each year.* Line 23, Spendable Cash, and Line 36, After Tax Cash Reversion, are each year discounted at the reversion factor which will discount cumulatively the sum of the Line 23 entries, and individually, Line 36, to $195,000, the present equity. This rate is obtained for each year by trial and error. But this is not as laborious as it may sound; in the example, for instance, no more than two trial rates were required for any year after the first year.

PROJECTIONS

YEAR	NET RESALE PRICE OR VALUE ESTIMATE (% OF BEGINNING)		GROSS INCOME (% OF BEGINNING)		VACANCY (% OF GR. POTENTIAL)		EXPENSES (%OF GR. POTENTIAL)	
1.	.99	.89	214,300 1.00 1.00		.25	.26	.33	.36
2.	.98	.88				.26	.33	.37
3.	.97	.87				.27	.33	.37
4.	.96	.86				.27	.33	.38
5.	.95	.85				.28	.33	.38
6.	.94						.34	
7.	.93						.34	
8.	.92						.35	
9.	.91						.35	
10.	.90						.36	

DEPRECIATION

DEPRECIABLE PROPERTY	COST	TYPE OF DEPRECIATION	REMAINING LIFE
BLDG	577,500	200% D.B.	40

MORTGAGES

MORTGAGE BALANCE OR %	RATE	TERM
.70	.095	20

GENE DILMORE, MAI–SREA–ASA

Figure 11.1A

CASH FLOW PROJECTION AND RATE OF RETURN ANALYSIS

		0	1	2	3	4	5			
1	Price or Value Estimate	650,000	643,500	637,000	630,500	624,000	617,500			
2	Total Mortgages	455,000	446,988	438,180	428,499	417,856	406,157			
3	Equity	195,000	196,512	198,820	202,001	206,144	211,343			
4										
5	Gross Income		214,300	214,300	214,300	214,300	214,300			
6	Vacancy		53,575	53,575	53,575	53,575	53,575			
7	Effective Gross		160,725	160,725	160,725	160,725	160,725			
8	Expenses		70,719	70,719	70,719	70,719	70,719			
9	Net Income		90,006	90,006	90,006	90,006	90,006			
10	Overall Return		.138	.140	.141	.143	.144			
11	Debt Service		50,894	50,894	50,894	50,894	50,894			
12	Capital Improvements									
13	Cash Before Taxes		39,112	39,112	39,112	39,112	39,112			
14	Equity Dividend		.200	.199	.197	.194	.190			
15	Net Income		90,006	90,006	90,006	90,006	90,006			
16	Interest Payments		42,882	42,087	41,213	40,252	39,194			
17	Depreciation		28,875	27,431	26,060	24,757	23,519			
18	Cumulative Depreciation		28,875	56,306	82,366	107,123	130,642			
19	Taxable Income $[15-(16+17)]$		18,249	20,488	22,733	24,997	27,291			
20	Tax Loss to Carry Forward									
21	Prior Tax Loss Used in Year									
22	Income Taxes 50%		9,124	10,244	11,366	12,498	13,646			
23	Spendable Cash (13 −22)		29,988	28,868	27,746	26,614	25,466			
24	Sold: Add Depr. exceeding S/L		14,437	27,430	39,052	49,371	58,452			
25	Taxable		1.00	.96	.84	.72	.60			
26	Tax		7,218	13,166	16,402	17,774	17,536			
27	Book Value		621,125	593,694	567,634	542,877	519,358			
28	Total Actual Depreciation		6,500	13,000	19,500	26,000	32,500			
29	Mortgagee Participation									
30	Capital Gain (1 −27, −24 x 25)		7,938	16,973	30,062	45,576	63,071			
31	x 1/2 = Net Capital Gain		3,969	8,487	15,031	22,788	31,535			
32	Tax		1,984	4,243	7,516	11,394	15,768			
33	Or: Deduct Carry-Forward Losses									
34	Taxable Inc., Ordinary Rate									
35	Tax									
36	After Tax Cash Reversion (3−26, −32)		187,310	181,411	183,083	176,976	178,039			
37	INTERNAL RATE OF RETURN*		.11 $\frac{7}{8}$	.11 $\frac{7}{8}$	.130	.12 $\frac{5}{8}$	.130			
38	Profitability Index									

*The rate at which the discounted present worth of all cash flows plus reversion of terminal value at end of this year equals the initial investment.

GENE DILMORE, MAI−SREA−ASA

Figure 11.1B

CASH FLOW PROJECTION AND RATE OF RETURN ANALYSIS

		6	7	8	9	10			
1	Price or Value Estimate	611 000	604 500	598 000	591 500	585 000			
2	Total Mortgages	393 297	379 161	363 622	346 541	327 764			
3	Equity	217 703	225 339	234 378	244 959	257 236			
4									
5	Gross Income	214 300	214 300	214 300	214 300	214 300			
6	Vacancy	53 575	53 575	53 575	53 575	53 575			
7	Effective Gross	160 725	160 725	160 725	160 725	160 725			
8	Expenses	72 862	72 862	75 005	75 005	77 148			
9	Net Income	87 863	87 863	85 720	85 720	83 577			
10	Overall Return	.142	.144	.142	.143	.141			
11	Debt Service	50 894	50 894	50 894	50 894	50 894			
12	Capital Improvements								
13	Cash Before Taxes	36 969	36 969	34 826	34 826	32 683			
14	Equity Dividend	.175	.170	.155	.149	.133			
15	Net Income	87 863	87 863	85 720	85 720	83 577			
16	Interest Payments	38 035	36 758	35 355	33 813	32 118			
17	Depreciation	22 343	21 226	20 164	19 156	18 198			
18	Cumulative Depreciation	152 984	174 210	194 374	213 530	231 728			
19	Taxable Income	27 485	29 879	30 201	32 751	33 261			
20	Tax Loss to Carry Forward								
21	Prior Tax Loss Used in Year								
22	Income Taxes	13 742	14 940	15 100	16 376	16 630			
23	Spendable Cash	23 227	22 029	19 726	18 450	16 053			
24	Sold: Add Depr. exceeding S/L	66 356	73 144	78 870	83 588	87 348			
25	Taxable	.48	.36	.24	.12	0			
26	Tax	15 925	13 166	9 464	5 015	0			
27	Book Value	497 016	475 790	455 626	436 470	418 272			
28	Total Actual Depreciation	39 000	45 500	52 000	58 500	65 000			
29	Mortgagee Participation								
30	Capital Gain (1 –27, –24 x 25)	82 133	102 378	123 445	144 999	166 728			
31	x 1/2 = Net Capital Gain	41 067	51 189	61 723	72 500	83 364			
32	Tax	20 533	25 595	30 861	36 250	41 682			
33	Or: Deduct Carry-Forward Losses								
34	Taxable Inc., Ordinary Rate								
35	Tax								
36	After Tax Cash Reversion (3–26 –32)	181 245	186 578	194 053	203 694	215 554			
37	INTERNAL RATE OF RETURN*	.13¼	.13¼	.135	.13⅝	.135			
38	Profitability Index								

*The rate at which the discounted present worth of all cash flows plus reversion of terminal value at end of this year equals the initial investment.

GENE DILMORE, MAI–SREA–ASA

Figure 11.1C

CASH FLOW PROJECTION AND RATE OF RETURN ANALYSIS

		11	12	13	14	15		
1	Price or Value Estimate	578 500	572 000	565 500	559 000	552 500		
2	Total Mortgages	307 124	284 435	259 495	232 079	201 943		
3	Equity	271 376	287 565	306 005	326 921	350 557		
4								
5	Gross Income	214 300	214 300	214 300	214 300	214 300		
6	Vacancy	55 718	55 718	57 861	57 861	60 004		
7	Effective Gross	158 582	158 582	156 439	156 439	154 296		
8	Expenses	77 148	79 291	79 291	81 434	81 434		
9	Net Income	81 434	79 291	77 148	75 005	72 862		
10	Overall Return	.139	.137	.135	.134	.132		
11	Debt Service	50 894	50 894	50 894	50 894	50 894		
12	Capital Improvements							
13	Cash Before Taxes	30 540	28 397	26 254	24 111	21 968		
14	Equity Dividend	.113	.105	.091	.078	.067		
15	Net Income	81 434	79 291	77 148	75 005	72 862		
16	Interest Payments	30 254	28 206	25 954	23 479	20 758		
17	Depreciation	17 289	16 424	15 603	14 823	14 082		
18	Cumulative Depreciation	249 018	265 442	281 045	295 868	309 949		
19	Taxable Income	33 891	34 661	35 591	36 703	38 022		
20	Tax Loss to Carry Forward							
21	Prior Tax Loss Used in Year							
22	Income Taxes	16 946	17 330	17 796	18 352	19 011		
23	Spendable Cash	13 594	11 067	8 458	5 759	2 957		
24	Sold: Add Depr. exceeding S/L							
25	Taxable							
26	Tax							
27	Book Value	400 982	384 558	368 955	354 132	340 051		
28	Total Actual Depreciation	71 500	78 000	84 500	91 000	97 500		
29	Mortgagee Participation							
30	Capital Gain (1 −27, −24 x 25)	177 518	187 442	196 545	204 868	212 449		
31	x 1/2 = Net Capital Gain	88 759	93 721	98 272	102 434	106 224		
32	Tax	44 380	46 860	49 136	51 217	53 112		
33	Or: Deduct Carry-Forward Losses							
34	Taxable Inc., Ordinary Rate							
35	Tax							
36	After Tax Cash Reversion (3−26, −32)	226 996	240 705	256 869	275 704	297 445		
37	INTERNAL RATE OF RETURN*	.13 5	.13 3/8	.13 1/4	.13 1/8	.13		
38	Profitability Index							

*The rate at which the discounted present worth of all cash flows plus reversion of terminal value at end of this year equals the initial investment.

GENE DILMORE, MAI–SREA–ASA

Figure 11.1D

As may be seen, under the given assumptions, the optimum resale period would be between the 8th and 11th years; from the 11th year, the return rate declines steadily.

Line 38, Profitability Index, is Present Worth of Equity divided by Actual Equity Investment. This is for use when the cost of investment and the return rate are given. The cash flows are discounted by this rate, rather than by a trial and error rate using present equity as target. This results in an indication of the entrepreneur's profit on the development.

Lines 10 and 14 are given for comparative purposes only. In my opinion, after the first year, these "rates" are meaningless; the internal rate of return is the only rate which properly discounts *all* incomes to present worth.

A good case may be made for the use of monthly discount factors, but in the example I have used annual factors because I feel that the typical investor only accounts once a year for his year's net profit or loss on an investment, and only calculates his return annually, even though he is receiving the income monthly. The monthly factors, therefore, would probably be mathematically more correct, but I am basically trying to conform with what appears to be market practice. Since the market is constantly becoming more sophisticated, monthly discount factors may quite possibly come into widespread use in the fairly near future.

Capital Cost Rate of Return

An alternative method of rate of return calculation has been suggested by Robert H. Baldwin.[1] Using a "cost of capital" rate, the cash flows are first compounded forward to the year under consideration, to give future worth of all cash flows, plus any reversion at that point. Then the cumulative future worth is divided by the beginning equity, if a single investment is involved, or by the equity plus present worth of any subsequent investments discounted at the same rate.

From this ratio the rate of return is then extracted, either by interpolation in the present worth tables, or by direct calculation.

To illustrate, suppose in the foregoing example that the return is sought, assuming sale at the end of 5 years. Using the internal rate of return, the indicated rate was 13%. Applying Baldwin's method, however, and using a capital cost rate at the mortgage interest rate of 9.5%, results as shown on the following page.

This method, therefore, indicates a rate 13/16% lower than the internal rate of return for the same period. When a valid basis is available for assignment of a capital cost rate, or reinvestment rate (such as a firm's overall earnings rate), this procedure is probably the most accurate measure of rate of return. It also properly accounts for the deferment factor in later additions to investment, by discounting these subsequent investments back to present worth and adding to the original investment.

When using such processes, the appraiser should not let an impressive array of calculations mislead him with respect to the degree of accuracy involved: the final result is still an estimate, and, as such, subject to error.

---

[1] Robert H. Baldwin, "How to Assess Investment Proposals," *Harvard Business Review,* May-June 1959.

Year	Spendable Cash	Compounded For	Future Worth Factor	Future Worth
1	$29,988	4 yrs.	1.437661	$43,113
2	28,868	3 "	1.312932	37,902
3	27,746	2 "	1.199025	33,268
4	26,614	1 "	1.095	29,142
5	25,466	0 "	1.0	25,466
5	Reversion			
	178,039	0 "	1.0	178,039

Future Worth of Incomes and Reversion. . . . . $ 346,930
Present Worth of Equity . . . . $ 195,000

$$\frac{346,930}{195,000} = 1.779128$$

Calculating return directly:

$\frac{\log\ 1.779128}{5}$; converted to antilog = 1.1221255

Rate of Return = approx. <u>12 3/16%</u>

XII

Capitalization Rate
Selection: How Rates of Return
Are Derived from the Market

$\mathbf{I}$n the derivation of capitalization rates, the following are the most widely used techniques:

COMPARATIVE METHOD, which derives a rate of overall net return from analysis of income for comparable sale properties.

BUILT-UP RATE, which contemplates adding a "safe" rate, a rate for allowance for risk, a rate for non-liquidity, and a rate for burden of management to synthesize a real estate interest rate.

BAND OF INVESTMENT METHOD, which adds a weighted mortgage rate and a weighted equity rate for a total interest rate.

THE McLAUGHLIN METHOD, which is a refinement of the band of investment method, weighting the mortgage rate in accordance with the actual debt service expected. The net effect of this method is to remove the entire mortgage payment portion from the estimated rate, leaving all other variables to the single straight line equity rate. The obverse of this method is the Cash Flow Analysis, testing a previously derived value indication.

ELLWOOD PROCESS: This method further refines the band of investment method and also accounts for equity increment and for anticipated total loss or gain in value over the projected income period, reducing the forecast period from total economic life of improvements to a more manageable ten or fifteen year income projection period, at the end of which reversion of the equity is assumed.

This is a rate selection method, not a capitalization method. The weighted portions of the capitalization rate are synthesized into a single rate which is used to process the income by applying the property residual technique, using the regular annuity method of capitalization.

A drawback of the process as usually applied, is the projection of an average income. Because of the varying effect of a discount as applied to different years, such averaging can misstate the value. When the income fluctuation is reasonably predictable, the problem can best be solved by simply discounting separately each year's income.

The following example illustrates the principle, assuming incomes as shown, averaging $5,000 per year, discounted at 9%:

Discounting Incomes Separately:

YR.	INCOME	P. W. FACTOR	P.W.
1	$ 8,000	.917431	$ 7,339
2	6,000	.841680	5,050
3	5,000	.772183	3,861
4	4,000	.708425	2,834
5	2,000	.649931	1,300
Total	$25,000		$20,384

Discounting the Average Income:

$5,000 average income x P. W. of 1
per annum factor   3.889651
                                    = $19,488

Averaging the projected income, in this case, understates the value by $896, or 4.6%.

Differences in Methods:

The comparative method, supplemented by the Ellwood Process, is the rate selection method advocated in this work, as this method is based on actual and current market activity.

The Built-Up Method is not used by investors in the income property market, and is therefore not a reliable market indicator.

The Band of Investment Method was a major contribution to the capitalization process, based on the fact that most income properties do carry mortgages of ascertainable ratios and interest rates. This technique helped to eliminate part of the desired factor from the judgment area, placing it in the given data area, thereby narrowing the range within which judgment must operate.

This method of capitalization rate selection, while a step in the right direction, has three flaws: (1) The failure to assign a limited life to the mortgage is obvious, the mortgage interest rate being, in effect, weighted in perpetuity; (2) the second fallacy, the failure to assign a finite life to equity return, is a less noticeable element, as is (3) the failure to account for equity increment.

The first omission was rectified by Frank J. McLaughlin, (*Appraisal Journal,* Oct. 1959), and the second and third were remedied by L. W. Ellwood (*Ellwood Tables,* 1959). In McLaughlin's refinement of the band of investment, he uses for the weighted mortgage rate the constant amortization factor for the term of mortgage applicable.

For example: Assuming a mortgage interest rate of 6% and a mortgage ration of 2/3, mortgage term of 15 years, the monthly constant payment factor of the mortgage portion is .008439 (this factor is used because actual payments are normally paid monthly). Multiplying by twelve, gives an annual constant of .101268. Multiplying this by 2/3 (the mortgage ratio) gives a weighted rate for the mortgage portion of the capitalization rate of .067512.

This is the equivalent of deducting the actual mortgage payment before capitalization. For the equity portion of the rate Mr. McLaughlin used the conventional band of investment method: 1/3 equity times 12% equity return gives a weighted equity rate of 4%, resulting in a total capitalization rate of .107512.

Study of the year-by-year returns reflected by this method indicates that something is still lacking in the process. Since the equity is constantly increasing by the amount of annual mortgage amortization, the income as a percentage of current investment is constantly diminishing. The fallacy involved in the assumption of either a decreasing or increasing interest rate (ratio of interest to *current* invested capital) may be clearly seen by supposing a sale at any time before the end of the economic life of the property, whereupon the interest rate must be immediately adjusted to conform with the stated current value.

Capital recapture as such is not provided for in this method, the one rate for equity yield being adjusted to account for any other factors such as economic life. Amortization and recapture in this method are generally assumed to balance out.

While the McLaughlin Method uses the mortgage amortization in the weighted mortgage portion of the capitalization rate, it does not make allowance in the final rate selection for the same amortization in its increment to the value. This problem, along with that of projecting a specific period of life for the investment, was undertaken by L. W. Ellwood.

This method of rate selection accounts for reversion of the enhanced equity after a stated period of income projection. Depreciation, or future value decline, is handled as a lump sum deduction (or addition for appreciation) at the end of the income projection period, being weighted in the overall capitalization rate.

Net Return as Indicator:

The overall net return rate derived from comparable sales furnishes the best value indicator available, as it embraces so many factors which otherwise would require separate accounting. This rate is then subject to a minimum of adjustments, as described in Chapter VIII.

The extraction of overall rates makes no implications as to recapture or economic life. It simply states the ratio of earnings to price, and is a convenient unit of comparison. It is not recommended that the overall rate be artificially fragmented into property interest rate and recapture rate, as this does not simulate the reasoning of the market. The only further breakdown of the overall rate should be, when possible, separation of mortgage and equity rates, a separation which does occur in the market.

If the comparable sale property is financed, the equity dividend can usually be found, for example: With a sale at $140,000, carrying a mortgage of $112,000 at 7% for 20 year term; net income before depreciation of $15,000.

Net income	$15,000
Less debt service (annual factor for 7%, 20 years)	10,430
Equity Dividend	$ 4,570

$4,570
$28,000=16.3% Equity Dividend

Equity *yield,* or total return on equity cannot be known until resale of the property.

Short-Cut for Overall Rate:

A short cut for derivation of overall rates of sales may be applied as follows:

When a number of fairly similar sale properties are accumulated, in the same property class, and their net income computed: The net operating ratio indicated may be used on a comparable sale for which the net is unknown, adjusting upward or downward for appreciable differences; then divide the net income ratio indicated by the other comparables, by the gross annual multiple, giving the overall rate, for example: Gross annual multiple of 6; net before depreciation indicated at 48%. .48/6 = .08 overall rate of return.

What Is Capitalized?

In the application of a return rate to an income stream, there are five sources from which the income may be generated:

(1) Net spendable cash after taxes
(2) Tax savings
(3) Equity increment from amortization
(4) Equity increment from appreciation
(5) Refinancing

It is evident that gross and net income fluctuate yearly; that tax savings also fluctuate, varying with changing depreciation allowances and with changing interest charges; and that equity increment or any refinancing profit is deferred until resale or refinancing.

For these reasons it is advocated that (1) after-tax net equity yield is the only meaningful measure when counseling the investor, that (2) the yield acceptable to that client is the relevant rate, and that (3) end-of-projection choices (resale, refinancing, trading, or retention) should be predicated, and that (4) each year's after-tax net should be discounted separately, following some form of Discounted Cash Flow analysis, as illustrated in Chapters XI and XVIII.

Despite its entrenched niche in the lithescent tradition of appraising, the oft-stated conception of the appraiser's function, "to observe and report," is no longer adequate to describe the function of the advanced appraiser, and certainly not that of the consultant. The appraiser who serves his proper function in the decision-making process no longer merely holds up a mirror to the market.

In practically all instances of employment of the wrong value calculus by the market, either in paying or lending too much, or in accepting too little for property, an appraiser has supplied a value estimate on the basis of which the mistaken action was taken.

It is no longer true that "appraisers do not make value," when it is quite customary for investors in both the equity and mortgage sector, to make their decisions depending heavily upon a value estimate from an appraiser. In the valuation of investment properties, it should be the appraiser's function to help guide his client in making better-informed business decisions. In doing this, he should be aware that his conclusions will have an impact on the market which he is analyzing.

XIII

The Ellwood Process
as a Method of Market
Data Analysis

$\mathbf{T}$he principle of deriving value from interest income was stated by Bohm-Bawerk, in 1884 (Eugen von Bohm-Bawerk, *Capital and Interest,* Vol. II, Book IV, pp 259-289), when he characterized present goods as being the equivalent of future goods except for an agio, or premium representing the discounted interest.

Irving Fisher (*The Theory of Interest,* 1930, pp. 14–15) explicitly formulated the concept that present value derived from discounted future interest income, rather than income being a product of capital value.

The major modification to capitalization rate selection practice has been the Ellwood process. It is assumed that the reader is familiar with the basic process of capitalization rate synthesis; some applications to market data analysis will be discussed.

Overall Rate:

Rejection of the straight line capitalization concept does not mean abandoning use of the overall rate of return, which is considered to constitute a ratio of present earnings to price, with no assumptions necessary as to economic life and depreciation. The Ellwood rate is a composite of mortgage and equity rates, but is based on the level annuity method of capitalization.

135

Analyzing for Yield:

One objective of a sale analysis may be to solve for "Y," the equity yield. A first approximation may be derived from the McLaughlin band of investment method, followed by interpolation for the specific Ellwood yield factor. (All page number references in this section refer to L. W. Ellwood, *Ellwood Tables,* 2nd edition, 1967, American Institute of Real Estate Appraisers):

Assumptions: A comparable sale at $150,000, with mortgage $100,000 for 20 years @ 6%. Net income is $15,000. R, or overall rate (dividing net income by sale price), is 10%.

Equity 1/3 x - - - - - - -   =   - - - - - - -
Mortgage 2/3 x .08604 (annual constant)
                                     =   .05736
          Overall Rate   .10000

Weighted and unweighted equity rates are unknowns, which may be completed by subtraction and division: Subtract weighted mortgage rate from overall rate (.04264). Divide this by 1/3 (.12792). This approximated yield, therefore, is .12792. This rate is then tested with the Ellwood process, allowing an estimated 10% total anticipated value decline over a 10 year projection period (page 247):

Y		.12792
-mc	(2/3 x .0632)	.0362
r		.09172
+dep x $1/s_n$	(.10 x .0543)	.00543
R		.09715

Since the result is a little low, Y is taken as 13%. (Remember that R is an overall return, and cannot be used in a land or building residual, as a portion of the 10% consists of recapture. The result would penalize the property value, as that portion would be deducted twice.)

Or, Y may be determined exactly, by applying the Ellwood steps in reverse:

R	.10000
- dep	.00543
= r	.09457
+ mc	.03620
= Y	.13077

Analyzing for Anticipated Depreciation:

On occasion, the problem with a comparable sale may be that we want to ascertain the probable amount of future depreciation, or total value decline, which is reflected in the sale. Our objective then, is to solve for depr. using the Ellwood formula:

$$Y - mc = r; \quad depr = \frac{R - r}{1/s_n}$$

Assume a comparable sale at $140,000, net income of $15,000 (R = .107), financing of 70% for 20 years at 7.5%. We believe an equity yield of 15% to be applicable, and want to ascertain the probable value decline over a 10 year projection period reflected in this transaction. We substitute in the equation, as follows (page 249):

$$
\begin{array}{lll}
Y & & .15000 \\
-mc & (.7 \times .0691) & .04837 \\
r = & & .10163
\end{array}
$$

Substituting: $\dfrac{.107 - .10163}{.0493} = 11\%$

We find, therefore, that an anticipated decline of total value of 11% over the 10 year projection period is consistent with the other facts of the transaction.

The Ellwood method of lump sum depreciation projection can also be used to account for an anticipated amount of required remodeling expense by simply adding this estimate to the depreciation estimate, or substituting it therefore, if the remodeling is considered to recoup all depreciation.

Declining Income

Where a declining income is anticipated, the income can most easily be processed by conversion to the equivalent regular annuity; in this manner, no adjustment need be fudged or guessed at, or applied to other factors in the valuation formula than the income. This conversion may be made by use of the following equation:

$$
\frac{(d - kn)a_n + \left[\dfrac{k}{Y}(N - a_n)\right]}{a_n} = \text{Equivalent Level Annuity}
$$

in which:

d = 1st period income
k = decline per period
N = # of period

a_n = PW of 1 per period
Y = rate of yield

Assuming an income beginning at $15,000, and declining at $500 per year, and assuming a yield rate of 9% and a projection period of 10 years, the equivalent level annuity if found by substitution as follows (page 212):

$$
\frac{[\$15,000 - (\$500 \times 10)](6.417658) + \left[\dfrac{500}{.09}(10 - 6.417658)\right]}{6.417658} = \frac{84,078}{6.417658} = \$13,101
$$

This is the equivalent regular annuity figure which may then be capitalized by the regular Ellwood process.

Analyzing for Value with Mortgage Ratio Unknown:

The Ellwood process provides a convenient method for estimating value when the amount of mortgage is known but the ratio to price or value is unknown. Assume a property with mortgage of $112,000, interest rate of 7%, term of 20 years, with net income of $15,000, equity yield of 12%, and estimated total property value decline of 15% over a 10 year projection period.

The steps are: (1) Obtain mortgage coefficient, (2) Multiply this times amount of mortgage; add total to income, (3) Capitalize at $Y + dep\ 1/s_n$. Indicated value is obtained as follows by substitution (page 249):

C =	.0459 x $112,000 =	$ 5,141
+ Income		15,000
Equivalent income		$20,141
Y		.12
+dep		.0085
R rounded		.1285 = 13%

$$\$20,141/.13 = \$155,000$$

Analyzing Offering

Assume an offering of a property at $950,000. The property has financing at 60% for 15 years, with 7.5% interest rate, gross income is $200,000; net $100,000. If equity yield of 15% is desired and provision for total value decline of 20% over a 10 year projection period, then (page 243):

Y	.15
-mc (.6) (.0652)	.0391
r	.1109
+dep (.20) (.0493)	.0099
R	.1208

$$\$100,000/.1208 = \$828,000$$

Although the property shows an overall return of 10.5% on the offering price, the client is advised not to purchase unless the price can be reduced to $828,000 as he cannot otherwise obtain an equity yield of 15%.

Analyzing Alternative Offerings:

Assume your client is interested in two alternative investments, both of which appear approximately equally desirable to him. You are asked to select the better investment of the two.

Property A is an eight unit apartment, average quality, carpets, drapes, all electric kitchens, individual air conditioners, two-bedroom unit, off street parking, building in good condition. Property has financing of $49,500 at $410 per month = $4,920 per year. Rentals are $115 per unit per month, or a total of $11,040 per year. The leases are for one year. Offering price is $79,500.

Property B is a free standing store, with AAA tenant, 13 years of a 15 year lease to run, direct lease, with rent of $920 per month or $11,040 per year. The property has financing of $50,000, for 15 years at 6%. Offering price is $75,000. In both cases, a 10% value decline is anticipated over a 10 year projection period. Your analysis proceeds somewhat as follows:

Property A: Gross rental $11,040
              Net rental   (75%)   8,280

Testing by Ellwood Process at 12% equity yield: (Interpolating between 7.5% and 8%, page 249)

Y	.1200
-mc (.622) (.0394)	.0245
r	.0955
+dep x 1/s (.10) (.0570)	.0057
R	.1012

Note the difference between the results of the Ellwood process and regular band of investment process:

		Weighted rate
Mortgage	.622 x .0775	.0482
Equity	.378 x .12	.0454
		.0936

It may be seen, therefore, that the regular band of investment technique understates the net return by ¾%, even with provision in the Ellwood process for 10% value decline.

Property B:	Gross rental	$600 x 12	$7,200
	Net rental	(80%)	$5,760

Testing with the same equity yield of 12%: reading direct from table, page 343, r= .0862, which, even without provision for depreciation, is higher than the actual .08 received. Moving up the table, therefore, .10 is still too high, so we move to Y= .09.

Y	.0900
r (direct)	.0728
+dep x 1/sn (.10) (.0658)	.0066
R	.0794

Since this return is consistent with the overall return, it is evident that property B can produce an equity yield of only 9%, compared with the 12% available from property A.

The return of 12% to the equity, as indicated for property A, is clearly superior to that of property B. The other principal factor remaining to be considered is the 13 year lease versus eight 1-year leases. This, however, for the most part is accounted for in the estimate of effective gross rental. The client, therefore, is advised to select property A, if he finds a 12% equity yield desirable.

When Financing Terms Not Tabulated:

Often the appraiser needs to use the Ellwood Process with financing terms which are not tabulated. This problem may be simplified by using the following six steps in the necessary calculations. The series of computations may also serve as the work sequence for programming the process if a desktop or larger computer is available. Once this sequence of equations is programmed, the computer can complete the calculations in a fraction of a second, giving the appraiser the ability to use any number of alternative terms.

First, a reminder as to definitions:

f = annual constant mortgage payment

i = mortgage interest rate

$S_m^n = (1 + i)^n$ for mortgage period

$S_p^n = (1+i)^n$ for projection period

P = portion of mortgage paid off in projection period

SFF = sinking fund factor, for Y rate

C = mortgage coefficient

Y = equity yield

depr/appr = Value decline of *total property* over projection period; if minus, is appreciation or value increase

r = rate of return before adjustment for depr or appr

R = overall rate of return

The Six Steps:

(1) $\dfrac{i}{1 - \dfrac{1}{S_m^n}} = f$

(2) $\left(\dfrac{f}{i} - 1\right)\ (S_p^n - 1) = P$

(3) $\dfrac{Y}{(S_p^n - 1)} = SFF$

(4) $Y + P\,(SFF) - f = C$

(5) $Y - MC = r$

(6) $\dfrac{R - r}{SFF} = appr/depr$　(+ = depr; - = appr)

When Overall Rate Is the Unknown:

The foregoing calculations assume that depr or appr is the unknown sought. When R, or overall rate of return is the unknown, the following simple sequence of steps will give the answer:

    (M x f)
+ (Eq x Y)
- (M x P x SFF)
+ (depr x SFF) (or - appr x SFF)
= R

When Mortgage Period Is Unknown:

Occasionally, the annual constant, or total yearly mortgage payment, may be known, but the mortgage period unknown. In this case, the mortgage period may be obtained by following these two steps:

$$(1) \quad \frac{i}{f - i} = (1 + i)^n$$

$$(2) \quad \frac{\log (1 + i)^n}{\log (1 + i)} = n, \text{ or number of periods.}$$

This calculation may be easily made with the aid of a logarithm table, or even more easily if your calculator has a log key. The resulting figure for n may then be inserted in either of the previously described sequences.

XIV

Inferential Statistics

At this point, let us examine our position, preparatory to moving forward:

The Three Approach dogma has been found wanting. The appraiser must feel free to approach a valuation as circumstances indicate, rather than illogically forcing the valuation process to fit an institutionalized format. Appraisers and appraisal-oriented academicians should set the standards for theory and practice in their profession rather than silently allowing unknowledgeable clients and administrative personnel who are not appraisal-oriented to promulgate long-discredited valuation processes.

The Cost Approach is to be avoided, except where no other approach is available. Even then, only actually available and possible alternatives are properly considered, and the result is not claimed to be market value.

Rates of return may be obtained only in the market, and they may be analyzed logically by the Ellwood process. The traditional method of capitalization, however, using the residual techniques, was found to be incorrect.

Much wasted effort has been noted in adjusting sales to comparability. This problem may be mitigated to some extent by delimitation of the value range and by use of a base property technique in analyzing comparable sales.

A need is still felt, however, for a truly objective method of value analysis.

Why the Statistical Approach?

A logical, theoretically sound, and practical method of analysis is available, in the use of inferential statistics. Regression analysis as a method of valuation was used by G. C. Haas of the University of Minnesota in 1922 for a study of farm valuation. It has, therefore, been available for a long time, but this valuable tool has lain generally unused and disregarded by the appraisal profession while its obsessive pursuit of trinality stultified the development of logical and scientific processes of valuation.

An orthodox appraisal is, to a limited degree, already a statistical inference problem: A sample of observations (sales) is drawn, and from analysis of the sample, predictions are made as to actions in the population from which the sample is taken. It is proposed merely to extend this approach into a more scientific process by use of inferential statistics. The technical knowledge required can be obtained in any ordinary course in elementary statistics.

This chapter is not intended as a substitute for a course in elementary statistics, but as a review of the steps most pertinent to the appraisal process.

The linear regression process, with one independent variable, is discussed first; this process can be applied without a computer, by careful selection of the sale data. Many appraisal problems can be reduced to one remaining independent variable (square footage, gross income, or net income).

Gross income is used in the present example for apartments, and area in the example for houses. The square footage and sale price limits are considered part of the description of the sample, and no extrapolation should be made outside the sample limits.

In appraising a property in a neighborhood for which an equation has been computed, it is necessary merely to apply the equation to subject, if it has all the attributes listed for the sample. One or two minor variances can then be accounted for by orthodox adjustment. If the property varies substantially from the sample description, however, the equation should not be used.

The premises of this technique are that many variances can be eliminated by careful selection of comparables, and that the most difficult variables to monetize are building area and gross or net income. If, of course, a number of comparables of the same area, or same gross or net income, are available, then some other important characteristic may be selected as the independent variable.

This process also results in a useful by-product: When a sample of sales is selected, similar with regard to several major traits, one particular item (second bath, garage, air conditioning, etc.) may be analyzed, resulting in a specific assignable value increment for the particular variable.

The balance of this chapter is devoted to a brief review of the basic principles and techniques involved. Attention will be mainly concentrated on the particular statistical processes of most relevance to appraisal problems.

Terminology:

X: Unknown quantity, or the first of two paired scores.

$\overline{X}$: The arithmetic mean of a group of X's.

x: X - $\overline{X}$, or a given score minus the mean of the group from which it is taken.

Y: An unknown, or the second of paired scores.

$\overline{Y}$: The mean of a group of Y's.

y: Y - $\overline{Y}$, or the given score minus the mean of its group.

Y': A predicted value, or dependent variable.

N: The number of observations under consideration.

Σ: Summation symbol, meaning "the sum of."

a: Constant in a regression equation, a residual figure of the portion of Y' not accounted for by b constant or constants.

b: Slope of the regression line, or the amount of variability in Y' accounted for by the variability of a given independent variable.

r: The Pearson product-moment correlation coefficient, usually referred to as Pearson r, or the correlation coefficient. This term indicates the measure of correlation between a dependent variable and one or more independent variables. The greater the correlation, the greater the predicted deviation from the sample mean. If there is a perfect correlation, there is maximum deviation.

r^2: The square of the preceding term, known as the coefficient of determination. This is a better measure of correlation than r, as it amounts to the explained variation divided by total variation, reflecting the percentage of variation in Y' accounted for by variations in the independent variables.

$S_{y.x}$: Standard error of estimate. This is the equivalent of a standard deviation, with the same characteristics; that is, 68% of a group of normally distributed scores will lie in an area plus or minus one standard error from the mean.

Normal Distribution:

A normal curve is the shape most often assumed by a random distribution. A normal curve indicates the percentage of the normal distribution found within one, two, and three standard deviations of the mean of the distribution. 68.26% of scores are found to lie within one standard deviation plus or minus from the mean; 95.44% within two deviations plus or minus; and 99.74% within three standard deviations plus or minus.

The normal curve is asymptotic; that is, the tails of the curve approach but never touch the base line. It is a symmetrical, bell-shaped distribution, with maximum height at the mean. (See Figure 14.1.)

Central Position:

The principle measures of central position are the mean, the median, and the mode. The mean is the arithmetic average of the numbers under consideration.

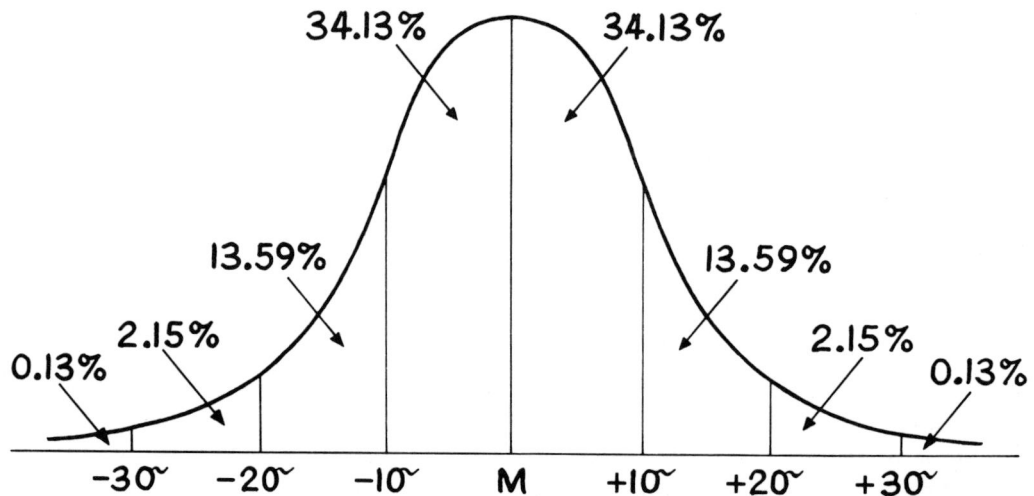

Figure 14.1 Normal Curve

$\overline{X} = \frac{\Sigma X}{N}$ or the sum of the scores divided by the number of scores. The characteristic of the mean, which is particularly utilized in regression analysis is that the sum of the squares of deviations from the arithmetic mean is less than the sum of squares of deviations about any other score.

Median: The point dividing halves of the number of items.

Mode: Item with greatest frequency.

Measures of Dispersion:

A given score has meaning only when it is defined as to both central tendency and a given measure of dispersion about the central tendency. There are several measures of dispersion.

Range: This is simply the overall spread of scores, measured by the highest score minus the lowest score plus one.

Mean deviation: Take the sum of the differences between the absolute values of the X's and the mean, and divide by the total number of scores. The absolute values are used because the algebraic sum of deviations from the mean would be O.

Variances-s^2: $\frac{\Sigma X^2}{N} - \overline{X}^2$ This term is of use principally, for our purposes, to show the source of the standard deviation which is simply its square root.

Standard deviation:
$$s = \sqrt{\frac{\Sigma (X - \overline{X})^2}{N}}$$

This formula represents the mean deviation method, by which the deviations of the X's from the mean are summed, the sum is squared, and divided by N, or the number of scores. The square root of the resulting figure is then taken.

Standard deviation (raw score method):

$$s = \sqrt{\frac{\Sigma X^2}{N} - \overline{X}^2}$$

This method of obtaining the standard deviation is usually a simpler calculation. It is found by taking the sum of the squares of the X's, dividing the sum by the number of scores, subtracting from this the square of the mean, and taking the square root of the resulting figure.

Two terms can easily cause miscalculation in the foregoing and similar formulas:

ΣX^2 and $(\Sigma X)^2$: The first is the sum of the squares of individual scores; the second is the square of the sums of the scores.

Standard error of estimate: Sy.x

This is a most useful measure in regression analysis, as it indicates the amount in dollars of the probable error attributable to the predicted value. It may be derived from any of several formulas, the following two of which are given here:

$$Sy.x = sy \sqrt{1 - r^2} \qquad Sy \cdot x = \sqrt{\frac{\Sigma Y^2 - a \Sigma Y - b \Sigma XY}{N}}$$

The first formula requires prior derivation of Sy, or the standard error of the Y. It also requires previous derivation of r^2 or the coefficient of determination. These values, however, are very often computed in the process of arriving at a point at which a standard error is desired.

The second formula, although requiring more computations, does not require prior computation of any figures except those necessary in preliminary ordering of the data.

It should be noted that the precision of the estimate can be heightened only at the cost of giving up some probability of being correct. The sample size (N) is the denominator of the error estimate; therefore, an increase of N, or number of observations, always reduces the error.

Degrees of Freedom:

The estimate of magnitude of dispersion in the population is made from the dispersion in the sample. The degrees of freedom consist of the number of observations, less the number of constraints or restrictions applied.

For example, in a simple regression (dependent variable plus one independent variable), there are two coefficients (a and b), so the degrees of freedom equals N minus 2. In a multiple regression with N = 40, and with 6 independent variables, there are 7 coefficients or constraints, so the degrees of freedom (N - M) equals 40 minus 7. This factor is needed for adjusting coefficients of correlation and estimates of error for small samples, and for analyses in which the number of constraints would materially change the estimate or correlation and dispersion.

Sampling:

The population is the total group from which a sample is selected. A sample is an attempted smaller scale replication of its population, with mean, median and variance approximating that of the population.

The sample design should be such that characteristics of the sample reflect to a reasonable degree those of the population. Doubling the sample size does not double the reliability of the estimate, as reliability increases in ratio to the square root of the sample size. For example, with varying sample sizes of 25 and 50: square root of 25 = 5. Square root of 50 = 7.07; therefore, doubling this sample size has increased the reliability of estimate by 41%.

In most applications of statistics, randomness is always desirable in the sample. In its use for appraising, however, this would not always be true. If analyzing for an equation to fit data in a large area, randomness would be desirable. If, however, analyzing for a specific property, and if a sampling of sales is being chosen with regard to valuation of a specific property, then the sample chosen should be as nearly like the subject as possible.

Correlation:

Simple linear correlation may be illustrated in a brief example: Assume the following pairs of X and Y observations:

X	Y
1	5
2	8
3	11
4	14
5	15

A chart is drawn for these data, using X as the measure on the ordinate, or X axis, and Y as the measure of the abscissa, or Y axis. The five pairs may then be spotted as shown in Figure 14.2.

After placement of the data on the scatter diagram, a straight line may be drawn through the dots in such a manner as to best fit the scattering of dots. This line, or slope, is the regression line; that is, the amount of vertical rise per unit of horizontal increase in the b coefficient in the straight line equation, $Y' = a + bX$.

This graphic representation illustrates the basic principle of correlation; the mathematical method of exact correlation computation will be discussed in Chapter XV.

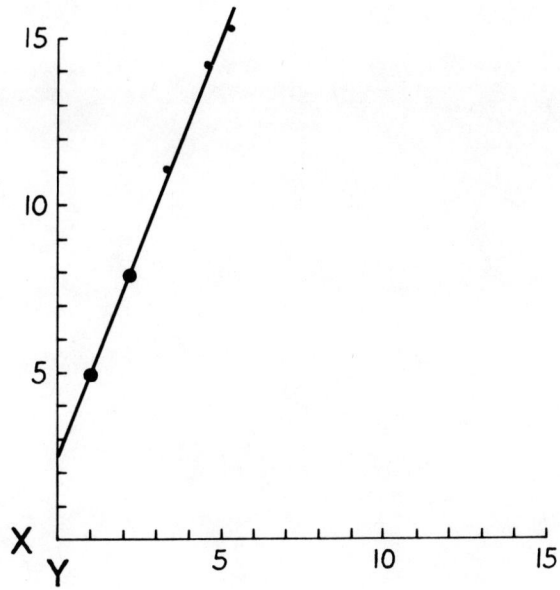

Figure 14.2 Simple Correlation

XV

Simple Linear Regression

The technique of simple linear regression, meaning a regression with one independent variable only, will be illustrated by means of a hypothetical example:

The objective is to compute the correlation and the nature of the relationship reflected in the following pairs of observations, each pair of observations being designated for convenience as X and Y:

X	Y
1	5
2	8
3	11
4	14
5	15

The data necessary for computation of the regression line for these figures are: X, Y, XY, X^2, Y^2, $\overline{X}, \overline{Y}, \overline{X}^2$, $\overline{Y}^2$, and N.

The data will be lined up as follows for computation:

X	Y	XY	X^2	Y^2
1	5	5	1	25
2	8	16	4	64
3	11	33	9	121
4	14	56	16	196
5	15	75	25	225

$\Sigma X = 15$ $\Sigma Y = 53$ $\Sigma XY = 185$ $\Sigma X^2 = 55$ $\Sigma Y^2 = 631$

$N = 5$ $\overline{X}^2 = 9$

$\overline{X} = 3$ $\overline{Y}^2 = 112.36$

$\overline{Y} = 10.6$

Both the correlation and the regression equation may be most easily computed, in eight simple steps, as follows:

Step 1: Standard error of estimate of X:

$$S_x = \sqrt{\frac{\Sigma X^2}{N} - \overline{X}^2}$$

$$Sx = \sqrt{\frac{55}{5} - 9} \quad = \quad \sqrt{2} \quad = \quad 1.4142$$

In this computation, we take the sum of the X^2s, divide it by N, or number of observations, subtract the square of the mean of the X's, and take the square root of the resulting figure.

Step 2: Standard error of estimate of Y:

$$S_y = \sqrt{\frac{\Sigma Y^2}{N} - \overline{Y}^2}$$

$$Sy = \sqrt{\frac{631}{5} - 112.36} \quad = \quad \sqrt{13.84} \quad = 3.72$$

This computation is the same as Step 1, except for using the Y observations instead of the X's. The Y^2's are summed, and divided by N; from the result is subtracted the square of the mean of the Y's, and the square root is taken of the resulting figure.

Step 3: Correlation coefficient:

$$r = \frac{\frac{\Sigma XY}{N} - \overline{X}\,\overline{Y}}{S_x S_y}$$

$$r = \frac{\dfrac{185 - (3)(10.6)}{5}}{(1.4142)(3.72)} \quad = \quad \frac{5.2}{5.26} \quad = \quad .99$$

This is the Pearson r, or coefficient of correlation. It is derived by summing the product of X and Y; dividing this by N or number of observations, subtracting the mean of X times mean of Y; dividing the total by the standard error of X times the standard error of Y. (The latter two figures are those derived in the first two steps.)

Step 4: Coefficient of Determination:

$$r^2 = .98$$

This is simply the square of the preceding figure. The coefficient of determination is a better measure of correlation than the correlation coefficient r, since it actually represents the percentage of variation in Y explained by variation in X.

Step 5: b constant: $\quad b = r \dfrac{S_y}{S_x}$

$$b = (.99)\frac{3.72}{1.4142} \quad = \quad (.99)(2.63) \quad = \quad 2.6$$

This is the coefficient by which X is multiplied in the regression equation. It is the same as the slope of the line in Figure 14.2; that is, the amount of unit increase in X required for a unit increase in Y.

The calculation uses only figures which were previously derived in Steps 1, 2, and 3: The correlation coefficient is multiplied by the standard error of Y divided by the standard error of X.

Step 6: a constant:

$$a = \overline{Y} - b\overline{X}$$
$$a = 10.6 - (2.6)(3) = 2.8$$

This is the constant or lump sum in the regression equation, which may be either a positive or a negative factor. It is the point on Figure 14.2 at which the regression line begins. It is computed by subtracting the product of b times the mean of X from the mean of Y.

Step 7: The Regression Equation:

$$Y' = a + bX$$
$$Y' = 2.8 + 2.6X$$

This is the final regression equation for predicted Y, or the dependent variable. The constant a is added to the product of b times X, the independent variable. The meaning of the equation is that the lump sum of 2.8 added to 2.6 times any of the X's will give the predicted Y corresponding to the given X.

Step 8: Standard Error of Estimate:

$$S_{y \cdot x} = \sqrt{\frac{\Sigma Y^2 - a \Sigma Y - b \Sigma XY}{N}}$$

$$S_{y \cdot x} = \sqrt{\frac{631 - [(2.8)(53)] - [(2.6)(185)]}{5}} = \sqrt{\frac{1.6}{5}}$$

$$= \sqrt{.32} = .57$$

The formula for the standard error of estimate has several alternate forms. The present one is used because it utilizes previously computed figures and gives an accurate calculation of the standard error.

In this formula, we sum the Y^2's, subtracting from this figure the product of a and the sum of Y, minus b times the sum of XY. The resulting figure is divided by N or number of pairs of observations; then the square root of this figure is taken.

The predicted Y will probably not vary from the actual Y more than one standard error in 68% of cases, two standard errors in 95% of cases, and three standard errors in 99.7% of cases.

One alternate formula for the standard error of estimate is: $S_y \sqrt{1 - r^2}$. This formula is simpler than the preceding one, being the multiplication of the standard error of Y by the square root of one minus the coefficient of determination. This is a convenient formula, since there are tables of the various functions of r and r^2. The computation requires only one multiplication. This formula was not used in the first example, as it is not quite as accurate as Step 8 for small figures.

Some of the other formulas in the preceding 8 steps have somewhat less complex alternate formulations, but the formulas selected for the 8 steps were chosen because they make maximum utilization of preceding computations.

Simple Regression, 12 Apartment Sales:

The practical application of the foregoing eight steps is illustrated below, with an actual sample consisting of twelve recent sales of garden apartments, ranging from 8 to 24 units, of average non-luxury construction, zero to five years old, and in a price range from $46,000 to $122,000.

These twelve actual sales may be analyzed without use of a computer by following the above-described eight steps which will result in a correlation coefficient, the coefficient of determination, the simple linear regression equation, and the standard estimate of error. The eight-step process may be followed below.

The data necessary for computation of the regression line for these figures are: X, Y, XY, X^2, Y^2, $\overline{X}$, $\overline{Y}$, $\overline{X}^2$, $\overline{Y}^2$, and N. The rent and price figures are divided by 1,000 for ease of calculation. The data will be lined up as follows for computation:

DATA FOR ANALYSIS

Gross Rent X	Price Y	XY	X^2	Y^2
9.552	68.000	649.536	91.241	4624
6.048	46.000	278.208	36.578	2116
6.750	53.000	357.750	45.562	2809
6.750	54.500	367.875	45.562	2970.25
4.860	37.500	182.250	23.620	1406.25
6.120	47.400	290.088	37.454	2246.75
8.100	65.000	526.500	65.610	4225
7.920	62.500	495.000	62.726	3906.25
7.020	50.000	351.000	49.280	2500
11.640	83.600	973.104	135.490	6988.96
15.960	122.000	1947.120	254.722	14,884
8.424	67.200	566.093	70.964	4515.84
99.144	756.700	6984.524	918.809	53,192.30

$N = 12$

$\overline{X} = 8.262$

$\overline{X}^2 = 68.261$

$\overline{Y} = 63.058$

$\overline{Y}^2 = 3976.353$

Step 1:

$$S_x = \sqrt{\frac{\Sigma X^2}{N} - \overline{X}^2}$$

$$S_x = \sqrt{\frac{918.809}{12} - 68.261} = \sqrt{76.567 - 68.261} = \sqrt{8.306} = 2.882$$

Step 2:

$$S_y = \sqrt{\frac{\Sigma Y^2}{N} - \overline{Y}^2}$$

$$S_y = \sqrt{\frac{53{,}192.30}{12} - 3976.353} = \sqrt{4432.692 - 3976.353}$$

$$= \sqrt{456.34} = 21.362$$

Step 3:

$$r = \frac{\dfrac{\Sigma XY}{N} - \overline{X}\,\overline{Y}}{S_x S_y}$$

$$r = \frac{\dfrac{6984.524}{12} - (8.262)(63.058)}{(2.882)(21.362)} = \frac{582.044 - 520.985}{61.565} = .99178$$

Step 4:

$$r^2 = .9836$$

Step 5:

$$b = r\frac{Sy}{Sx}$$

$$b = (.992)\frac{21.362}{2.882} = 7.353$$

Step 6:

$$a = \overline{Y} - b\overline{X}$$

$$a = 63.058 - (7.353)(8.262) = 2.308 = \$2,308$$

Step 7:

$$Y' = a + bX$$

$$Y' = \$2,308 + (7.353)(\text{Gross})$$

Step 8:

$$Sy \cdot x = \sqrt{\frac{\Sigma Y^2 - a\,\Sigma Y - b\,\Sigma XY}{N-M}} \quad \text{(Adjusting for degrees of freedom)}$$

$$Sy \cdot x = \sqrt{\frac{53,192.30 - [(2.308)(756.7)] - [7.353)(6984.524)]}{12-2}} =$$

$$\sqrt{\frac{88.641}{10}} = \sqrt{8.8641} = 2.977 = \$2,977$$

The conclusions drawn from the foregoing simple regression analysis are as follows:

The sale price of an apartment generally fitting the description of the sale properties, and in locations similar to those of the sale properties, may be predicted with the equation: $2,308, plus 7.353 times gross annual rent.

The variation in the b factor (multiplier of gross) accounts for 98% of the variability in Y (sales price).

68% of the time the predicted sale price will fall within $2,977 of the actual sale price. 95% of the time predicted sale price will fall within $5,954 of the actual sale price. 90% of the time the predicted sale price will fall within $4,897 (1.645 standard errors), or 7.8% of the mean actual sale price.

The foregoing conclusions would tend to indicate that a considerable amount of effort is wasted in gathering and analyzing irrelevant data in the orthodox appraisal process.

Simple Regression, 15 Residential Sales:

The following example consists of 15 frame houses, all in the same neighborhood, in a size range of 922 to 1,373 square feet, in a price range of $10,200 to $18,250, with one-car carport, but with variances as to number of baths, ages, basements, and extras.

Simple Linear Regression, 15 Houses
(All figures divided by 1,000)

	Size X	Price Y	XY	X^2	Y^2
1	1.075	14.610	15.7058	1.1556	213.4521
2	.989	14.500	14.3405	.9781	210.2500
3	1.026	12.134	12.4495	1.0527	147.2340
4	1.054	11.600	12.2264	1.1109	134.5600
5	1.042	13.500	14.0670	1.0858	182.2500
6	1.144	13.100	14.9864	1.3087	171.6100
7	1.144	13.000	14.8720	1.3087	169.0000
8	1.225	15.600	19.1100	1.5006	243.3600
9	1.108	14.185	15.7170	1.2277	201.2142
10	1.080	13.950	15.0660	1.1664	194.6025
11	1.191	15.500	18.4605	1.4185	240.2500
12	1.373	18.250	25.0572	1.8851	333.0625
13	1.176	16.750	19.6980	1.3830	280.5625
14	.922	11.000	10.1420	.8501	121.0000
15	1.017	10.200	10.3734	1.0343	104.0400
	16.566	207.879	232.2717	18.4662	2946.4478

N = 15 $\overline{Y}$ = 13.8586
$\overline{X}$ = 1.1044 $\overline{Y^2}$ = 192.0608
$\overline{X^2}$ = 1.2197

Step 1:

$$S_x = \sqrt{\frac{\Sigma X^2}{N} - \overline{X}^2}$$

$$S_x = \sqrt{\frac{18.4662}{15} - 1.2197} = .1067$$

Step 2:

$$S_y = \sqrt{\frac{\Sigma Y^2}{N} - \overline{Y}^2}$$

$$S_y = \sqrt{\frac{2946.4478}{15} - 192.0608} = 2.0902$$

Step 3:

$$r = \frac{\frac{XY}{N} - \overline{XY}}{S_x S_y}$$

$$r = \frac{\frac{232.2717}{15} - (1.1044)(13.8586)}{(.1067)(2.0902)} = \frac{.1793}{.223} = .804$$

Step 4:

$$r^2 = .646$$

Step 5:

$$b = r\frac{S_y}{S_x}$$

$$b = (.804)\frac{(2.0902)}{(.1067)} = 15.75$$

Step 6:

$$a = \overline{Y} - b\overline{X}$$

$$a = 13.8586 - (15.75)(1.1044) = -3.5357$$

Step 7:

$$Y' = a + bX$$

$$Y' = \$3.536 + \$15.75 \text{ (Size)}$$

Step 8:

$$Sy \cdot x = \sqrt{\frac{\Sigma Y^2 - a\,\Sigma Y - b\,\Sigma XY}{N}}$$

$$Sy \cdot x = \sqrt{\frac{(2946.4478) - [(-3.536)(207.879)] - [(15.75)(232.2717)]}{15}}$$

$$= \sqrt{\frac{23.2286}{15}} \quad = \quad 1.546 \quad = \quad \$1,546$$

The conclusions drawn from the foregoing simple linear regression analysis are as follows:

The sale price of a residence in this neighborhood, and fitting the given general description, may be predicted with the equation: Price = -\$3536 + \$15.75 (Size).

The variation in the b factor (square footage) accounts for 65% of the variability in the sale price.

68% of the time the predicted sale price will fall within \$1,546 of the actual sale price. 95% of the time the predicted sale price will fall within \$3,092 of the actual sale price. 90% of the time the predicted sale price will fall within \$2,543 of the actual sale price, or 18% of the mean actual sale price.

A quite wide range of error is still indicated, but in actual practice, sale properties more similar may be selected. The houses in the present sample still have differences in number of baths, ages, basements, and extras. The sample was left random, except for exterior construction and carport, so that comparison may be more easily made with results of adding both to the sample size and to the number of independent variables, as illustrated in the chapter following.

XVI

Multiple Regression Analysis

$\mathbf{W}$e have seen how sale prices may be predicted (market value estimated) by use of simple linear regression, using only one independent variable. Multiple regression makes use of more than one independent variable. In this chapter, we will expand this approach, using first two independent variables, then three. Fifteen houses from the same group will be used, but without eliminating those of brick veneer construction, so that the comparative accuracy and reliability may be observed.

The data are first ordered, so that sums, squares, and cross products may be taken.

In the preceding chapter, square footage was the single independent variable. In this chapter, we will add age as a second variable, then construction as a third. Increasing precision in the value estimate will be noted as we add variables. (Precision is not enhanced indefinitely, however, by simply adding variables.)

The Adjustment Items are, in each case, N times the mean of the factor; for example, in the X^2 column, the adjustment item is $N(M^2)$.

If the steps in the computations are taken carefully and in sequence, it will be seen that this process really involves no more complex mathematics than a simple regression; it merely requires more arithmetic calculations.

The arithmetic can be simplified somewhat by coding some of the data; for instance dividing all figures for a variable by 1,000. The computations were left uncoded here, so that the basic process may be more easily observed.

Multiple Regression
15 Houses, 2 Independent Variables

Size X_1	Age X_2	Price X_0		X_1^2	X_2^2
1,075	10	14,610		1,155,625	100
989	12	14,500		978,121	144
1,026	12	12,134		1,052,676	144
1,054	15	11,600		1,110,916	225
1,042	16	13,500		1,085,764	256
1,144	15	13,100		1,308,736	225
1,144	13	13,000		1,308,736	169
1,225	8	15,600		1,500,625	64
1,108	12	14,185		1,227,664	144
1,080	18	13.950		1,166,400	324
1,191	7	15,500		1,418,481	49
1,122	12	15,833		1,258,884	144
1,339	3	21,500		1,792,921	9
1,519	0	26,500		2,307,361	0
1,392	5	20,300		1,937,664	25
Σ 17,450	158	235,812		20,610,574	2,022
Mean 1,163.333	10.533	15,720.80	Adjustment Item	20,300,155.03	1,664.161
			Adjusted Sums	310,418.97	357.839

	X_0^2	X_0X_1	X_0X_2	X_1X_2
	213,452,100	15,705,750	146,100	10,750
	210,250,000	14,340,500	174,000	11,868
	147,233,956	12,449,484	145,608	12,312
	134,560,000	12,226,400	174,000	15,810
	182,250,000	14,067,000	216,000	16,672
	171,610,000	14,986,400	196,500	17,160
	169,000,000	14,872,000	169,000	14,872
	243,360,000	19,110,000	124,800	9,800
	201,214,225	15,716,980	170,220	13,296
	194,602,500	15,066,000	251,100	19,440
	240,250,000	18,460,500	108,500	8,337
	250,683,889	17,764,626	189,996	13,464
	462,250,000	28,788,500	64,500	4,017
	702,250,000	40,253,500	0	0
	412,090,000	28,257,600	101,500	6,960
	Σ 3,935,056,670	282,065,240	2,231,824	174,758
Adjustment Items	3,707,153,289	274,327,881	2,483,808	183,801
Adjusted Sums	227,903,381	7,737,359	- 251,984	- 9,043

Solution of Three Simultaneous Equations

I. $\Sigma(X_1^2)b_1 + \Sigma(X_1 X_2)b_2 = \Sigma(X_0 X_1)$

II. $\Sigma(X_1 X_2)b_1 + \Sigma(X_2^2)b_2 = \Sigma(X_0 X_2)$

III. $a = M_0 - b_1 M_1 - b_2 M_2$

Substituting:

I. $(310,418.97)b_1 - (9043)b_2 = 7,737,359$

II. $(-9043)b_1 + (357.839)b_2 = -251,984$

(1) Divide I by coefficient of b_1 with sign changed, giving derived equation I'.

(2) Enter II, and under it I multiplied by coefficient of b_2 in equation I'. Add these 2 equations, eliminating b_1 and giving b_2.

(3) Substitute value of b_2 in I', giving b_1.

(4) Substitute value of b_2 and b_1 in III, giving a.

(5) $Xo = a + b_1 X_1 + b_2 X_2$.

(1) I' $-b_1 + (.02913)b_2 = 24.926$

(2) II $(-9,043)b_1 + (357.839)b_2 = -251,984$

$\qquad (9,043)b_1 - (263.423)b_2 = 225,389.268$

$\qquad\qquad\qquad 94.416b_2 = -26,594.732$

$\qquad\qquad\qquad\qquad b_2 = -281.694$

(3) I' $- b_1 + 8.206 \qquad = 24.926$

$\qquad\qquad b_1 \qquad = 16.72$

(4) $a = 15,720.80 - (16.72)(1163.333) - (-281.694)(10.533)$

$\quad a = -763.04$

(5) $X_0' = -\$763 + (\$16.72)(\text{Size}) - (\$282)(\text{Age})$

After computation of the regression equation, the degree of probable error and the amount of price variation "explained" by the equation are calculated as follows:

The equation is applied to each data item, giving X_0', the predicted sale price. This is subtracted from X_0, or actual price, giving d, the absolute difference. This is then squared. These totals are then processed as shown below, to give S_x, the Standard Error, and R^2, the coefficient of determination.

**Computations of Standard Error and
Coefficient of Determination**

(X_0' = predicted price; d = difference
between actual and predicted price.)

X_0	X_0'	d	d^2
14,610	14,391	219	47,961
14,500	12,389	2,111	4,456,321
12,134	13,008	874	770,884
11,600	12,630	1,030	1,060,900
13,500	12,147	1,353	1,830,609
13,100	14,135	1,035	1,071,225
13,000	14,699	1,699	2,886,601
15,600	17,463	1,863	3,470,769
14,185	14,379	194	37,636
13,950	12,219	1,731	2,996,361
15,500	17,177	1,677	2,812,329
15,833	14,613	1,220	1,488,400
21,500	20,779	721	519,841
26,500	24,635	1,865	3,478,225
20,300	21,101	801	641,601

$\overline{X}$ 15,721 Σd 18,393 Σd^2 26,569,663

Average Deviation = $1,226
= .078

$$Sx = \sqrt{\frac{\Sigma d^2}{N}} \quad = \$1,331$$

68% of time $1,331
95% of time $2,662
90% of time $2,189 or 14%

$$R^2 = 1 - \frac{\Sigma d^2}{\Sigma(X_0{}^2) - \frac{(\Sigma X_0)^2}{N}}$$

$$R^2 = 1 - \frac{26,569,663}{3,935,056,670 - \frac{55,607,299,340}{15}}$$

$$R^2 = .88$$

We will now add one variable to the analysis, using three independent variables consisting of Size, Age and Construction. Brick veneer is taken as 1, frame construction as 0.

Multiple Regression, 3 Independent Variables

Size X_1	Age X_2	Constr. X_3	Price X_0		X_1^2
1,075	10	0	14,610		1,155,625
989	12	0	14,500		978,121
1,026	12	0	12,134		1,052,676
1,054	15	0	11,600		1,110,916
1,042	16	0	13,500		1,085,764
1,144	15	0	13,100		1,308,736
1,144	13	0	13,000		1,308,736
1,225	8	0.5	15,600		1,500,625
1,108	12	0.5	14,185		1,227,664
1,080	18	0	13,950		1,166,400
1,191	7	0	15,500		1,418,481
1,122	12	1	15,833		1,258,884
1,339	3	1	21,500		1,792,921
1,519	0	1	26,500		2,307,361
1,392	5	1	30,300		1,937,664
Σ17,450	158	5	235,812		20,610,574
Mean 1,163.333	10.533	.333	15,720.80	Adjustment Item	20,300,155.03
				Adjusted Sum	310,418.97

	X_2^2	X_3^2	X_0^2	X_0X_1	X_0X_2
	100	0	213,452,100	15,705,750	146,100
	144	0	210,250,000	14,340,500	174,000
	144	0	147,233,956	12,449,484	145,608
	225	0	134,560,000	12,226,400	174,000
	256	0	182,250,000	14,067,000	216,000
	225	0	171,610,000	14,986,400	196,500
	169	0	169,000,000	14,872,000	169,000
	64	.25	243,360,000	19,110,000	124,800
	144	.25	201,214,225	15,716,980	170,220
	324	0	194,602,500	15,066,000	251,100
	49	0	240,250,000	18,460,500	108,500
	144	1	250,683,889	17,764,626	189,996
	9	1	462,250,000	28,788,500	64,500
	0	1	702,250,000	40,253,500	0
	25	1	412,090,000	28,257,600	101,500
Σ	2,022	4.500	3,935,056,670	282,065,240	2,231,824
Adjustment Item	1,664.161	1.663	3,707,153,289	274,327,881	2,483,808
Adjusted Sums	357.839	2.837	227,903,381	7,737,359	- 251,984

X_0X_3	X_1X_2	X_1X_3	X_2X_3
0	10,750	0	0
0	11,868	0	0
0	12,312	0	0
0	15,810	0	0
0	16,672	0	0
0	17,160	0	0
0	14,872	0	0
7,800	9,800	612.5	4
7,092	13,296	554	6
0	19,440	0	0
15,833	13,464	1,122	12
21,500	4,017	1,339	3
26,500	0	1,519	0
20,300	6,960	1,392	5

	X_0X_3	X_1X_2	X_1X_3	X_2X_3
Σ	99,025	174,758	6,538.5	30.000
Adjustment Items	78,525	183,801	5,810.8	52.612
Adjusted Sums	20,500	- 9,043	727.7	-22.612

Adjustment Items:

$N(M_1{}^2)$	$N(M_0M_1)$	$N(M_1M_3)$
$N(M_2{}^2)$	$N(M_0M_2)$	$N(M_2M_3)$
$N(M_3{}^2)$	$N(M_0M_3)$	
$N(M_0{}^2)$	$N(M_1M_2)$	

Estimating Equation: $X_0' = a + b_1X_1 + b_2X_2 + b_3X_3$

Solutions of Four Simultaneous Equations

(1)   Set down equation I, divide by coefficient of first term with sign changed.

(2)   Resulting equation, I' is set down below I.

(3)   Set down equation II.
      Multiply equation I by coefficient of second term in I'. Set products down below II.

(4)   Add these 2 equation, giving equation Σ_2, which cancels first term.

(5)   Divide Σ_2 by coefficient of first term with sign changed, giving equation II'.

(6)   Set down equation III.
      Multiply equation I by coefficient of third term of I'. Set products down below III.

(7)   Multiply equation Σ_2 by coefficient of second term of II'. Set down products below previous equation.

(8)   Add III and the 2 new equations, giving Σ_3, from which b_1 and b_2 have been eliminated.

(9)   Divide Σ_3 by coefficient of its first term giving III'.

(10)   Substitute b_3 (from III') in II', giving b_2.

(11)   Substitute b_2 and b_3 in I', giving b_1.

(12)   Substitute foregoing values in IV, giving a.

$$\text{I} \quad \Sigma(X_1{}^2)b_1 + \Sigma(X_1 X_2)b_2 + \Sigma(X_1 X_3)b_3 = \Sigma(X_0 X_1)$$

$$\text{II} \quad \Sigma(X_1 X_2)b_1 + \Sigma(X_2{}^2)b_2 + \Sigma(X_2 X_3)b_3 = \Sigma(X_0 X_2)$$

$$\text{III} \quad \Sigma(X_1 X_3)b_1 + \Sigma(X_2 X_3)b_2 + \Sigma(X_3{}^2)b_3 = \Sigma(X_0 X_3)$$

$$\text{IV} \quad a = M_0 - (b_1 M_1) - (b_2 M_2) - (b_3 M_3)$$

(1) I $(310{,}418.97)b_1 - (9{,}043)b_2 + (727.7)b_3 = 7{,}737{,}359$

(2) I' $-b_1 + .02913b_2 - .002344b_3 = -24.926$

(3) II $(-9043)b_1 + 357.839b_2 - 22.612b_3 = -251{,}984$

$9043b_1 - 263.423b_2 + 21.198b_3 = 225{,}389.268$

(4) Σ_2 $\qquad\qquad\qquad 94.416b_2 - 1.414b_3 = -26{,}594.732$

(5) II' $-b_2 + .01498b_3 = 281.676$

(6) III $(727.7)b_1 - (22.612)b_2 + 2.837b_3 = 20{,}500$

$-(727.7)b_1 + (21.197)b_2 - 1.706b_3 = -18{,}136.370$

$-1.415b_2 + 1.131b_3 = -2{,}363.630$

(7) $1.415\,b_2 - .021b_3 = -398.389$

(8) $(727.7)b_1 - (22.612)b_2 + (2.837)b_3 = 20{,}500$

$-(727.7)b_1 + (21.197)b_2 - (1.706)b_3 = -18136.370$

$(1.415)b_2 - (.021)b_3 = -398.389$

$\Sigma_3 \qquad\qquad 1.110b_3 = 1{,}965.241$

(9)   III' $b_3 = 1{,}770.487$

(10) $-b_2 + 26.522 = 281.676$
                  $b_2 = -255.154$

(11) $-b_1 - 7.433 - 4.150 = -24.926$
                      $b_1 = 13.343$

(12) $a = 15{,}720.80 - (13.343)(1163.333) - (-255.154)(10.533) - (1770.487)(.333)$
          $a = 2296.41$

$X'_0 = \$2{,}296 + \$13.34 \text{ (Sq. Ft.)} - \$255 \text{ (Age)} + \$1770 \text{ (If Brick Veneer)}$

Computation of Standard Error and
Coefficient of Determination

X_0	X'_0	d	d^2
14,610	14,086	524	274,576
14,500	12,429	2,071	4,289,041
12,134	12,923	789	622,521
11,600	12,531	931	866,761
13,500	12,116	1,384	1,915,456
13,100	13,732	632	399,424
13,000	14,242	1,242	1,542,564
15,600	17,482	1,882	3,541,924
14,185	14,902	717	514,089
13,950	12,113	1,837	3,374,569
15,500	16,399	899	808,201
15,833	15,973	140	19,600
21,500	21,163	337	113,569
26,500	24,329	2,171	4,713,241
20,300	21,360	1,060	1,123,600

$\bar{X}$ 15,721 Σd 16,616 Σd^2 24,119,136

Average Deviation $= \$1{,}108$
$= .070$

$$S_x = \sqrt{\frac{\Sigma d^2}{N}} = 1{,}268$$

$$R^2 = 1 - \frac{\Sigma d^2}{\Sigma(X_0^{\,2}) - \frac{(\Sigma X_0)^2}{N}}$$

$$R^2 = 1 - \frac{24{,}119{,}136}{3{,}935{,}056{,}670 - \frac{55{,}607{,}299{,}340}{15}}$$

$$R^2 = .894$$

Comparison of Results:

Results from regression analysis using different numbers of variables may be noted in the fifteen houses analyzed in Chapters XV and XVI, as follows:

	R^2	$Sy \cdot x$
One Independent Variable	.65	$1,546
Two Independent Variables	.88	$1,331
Three Independent Variables	.894	$1,268

In each instance, addition of a variable enhanced the accuracy and the reliability of the value estimate. Addition of more variables may be expected to further improve the estimate, with the condition that, with more variables, larger samples are also needed. (In the foregoing examples, the final results vary slightly from those obtained from a computer run, due to rounding of figures.)

Degrees of Freedom:

The concept of degrees of freedom was touched upon in Chapter XIV. At this point, it should be further noted that small samples, such as the previously discussed 15 houses, would in actual practice require an adjustment for the number of degrees of freedom lost. For example, in computing S y.x, the Standard Error of Estimate, for the sample of houses in Chapter XIV, the following adjustment would be necessary:

$$Sy \cdot x = \sqrt{\frac{\Sigma Y^2 - a \Sigma Y - b \Sigma XY}{N-M}}$$

(Reminder: M = number of coefficients)

$$= \sqrt{\frac{23.2286}{15 - 2}} = \$1,787$$

This, then, would be the adjusted standard error of estimate, rather than $1,546. For the three successive regressions, the adjusted Standard Errors would be respectively, $1,787, $1,488, and $1,481.

As the sample size approaches thirty, the distribution assumes a shape closer and closer to a normal distribution, so that, with a sample size of 30 plus the total number of variables (including the dependent variable), a normal distribution is approximated, so that the effect of the foregoing adjustment is minimal.

Isolating Value Determinants:

This technique may be applied to problems other than that of total value estimation, the most useful being isolation of individual value determinants.

For example, suppose your problem is estimation of damage to remainder of a number of residences by virtue of a street widening. When sufficient sales are available, a basic damage factor may be derived by simply running a regression analysis of your comparable sales, using depth of setback as one of the independent variables. The resulting estimating equation will contain a factor of "x dollars per foot of setback."

This average figure can then be used as the basis of a depth table, to give effect to the non-linear effect of increasing encroachment.

The author has used this process to extract a number of "market data adjustments," to determine the actual amount assigned by the market to a specific value factor. For example, differential for central heating over floor furnace heating, age of improvements, time of sale, corner influence, distance from 100% corner, high rise vs. low rise, distance from bus stop, etc. When applying a regression analysis, it should be remembered that there is a weakness in the technique in that it is a linear analysis, that is, changes are assumed to increase in a straight line, while, obviously, some factors, such as size, do not take effect in a linear manner. This can be rectified to some extent by using the logarithms of such data rather than the actual data.

Regression Analysis with More than Three Variables:

The simultaneous equations needed for a multiple regression analysis with 4 independent variables are as follows:

$$\Sigma(X_1{}^2)b_1 + \Sigma(X_1X_2)b_2 + \Sigma(X_1X_3)b_3 + \Sigma(X_1X_4)b_4 = \Sigma(X_0X_1)$$
$$\Sigma(X_1X_2)b_1 + \Sigma(X_2{}^2)b_2 + \Sigma(X_2X_3)b_3 + \Sigma(X_2X_4)b_4 = \Sigma(X_0X_2)$$
$$\Sigma(X_1X_3)b_1 + \Sigma(X_2X_3)b_2 + \Sigma(X_3{}^2)b_3 + \Sigma(X_3X_4)b_4 = \Sigma(X_0X_3)$$
$$\Sigma(X_1X_4)b_1 + \Sigma(X_2X_4)b_2 + \Sigma(X_3X_4)b_3 + \Sigma(X_4{}^2)b_4 = \Sigma(X_0X_4)$$
$$a = M_0 - b_1M_1 - b_2M_2 - b_3M_3 - b_4M_4$$

Comparison with the equations for a regression with 3 independent variables will show that no procedural change is necessary; the appropriate terms involving X_4 and b_4 are merely added to each equation, and one equation added.

The process for solving a regression equation with 4 or more independent variables is simply an extension of the processes already demonstrated, and will not be illustrated here for two reasons: (1) It would be mostly repetition, as the procedure for expanding, say, or from 3 to 4 independent variables, or from 4 to 5, etc., is exactly the same as that for expanding from 2 to 3 independent variables. (2) Each addition of variables and sample data increases the amount of simple arithmetic considerably. When working a regression with 5 or 6 independent variables, the appraiser is inefficiently using his time on a great number of simple computations when, especially in view of the declining costs of computers and computer time, the calculations may be more cheaply performed on a computer.

Worksheet:

Figure 16.1 illustrates a convenient format for a multiple regression worksheet. Figures for "Construction" are 0 for frame, 1 for brick veneer. The ranges and the composite property description are useful in evaluating the applicability of the equation to the subject property.

An apparent anomaly will be noted here; a deduction for basement. This is the result of multicollinearity, or the correlation of two or more of the independent variables with each other as well as with the dependent variable. In this case, basements are correlated with age, as well as with architectural style, which were not used as variables. In an instance of this sort, it must be remembered that the "pluses and minuses" are applicable only in conjunction with the balance of the equation, and only with subjects matching the data properties.

VESTAVIA
ALL BRICK VENEER, ALL AIR CONDITIONED

No.	Size	Age	Car Storage	Basement	Baths	Extras	Price
	X_1	X_2	X_3	X_4	X_5	X_6	X_0
1	1618	0	2	0.5	3	5	$35,400
2	1808	14	3	0	2	2	24,500
3	1566	4	1	0.5	2	0	24,850
60	1682	7	2	0.5	2	2	26,500

$$X_0 =$$

a	5,930	$\overline{X_0}$ = $29,382
$+b_1$	13.16	Sy · x = $608
$-b_2$	657	
$+b_3$	619	90% Probability = $1,000
$-b_4$	1,524	R^2 = .932
$+b_5$	667	
$-b_6$	1,091	Average Deviation = .051

Figure 16.1

Range of Data:		Composite:
Price	$20,750 - $45,000	$29,382
Size	1,250 - 2,610 S/F	1,772
Age	0 - 16	8
Car	0 - 3	2
Bsmt.	0 - 1	0.5
Baths	2 - 3.5	2.35
Extras	0 - 8	3
All B. V., All A. C.		B. V., A. C.

Figure 16.1 (continued)

Sample and Prediction Limits:

In drawing inferences from a sample, no prediction should be made outside the limits of the sample. In a sample of houses between 1,500 and 2,300 square feet in liveable area, extrapolation for a house of 2,600 square feet would be improper. The same would be true of the other descriptive characteristics of the sample properties.

Conclusions:

Regression analysis is the most objective approach to the valuation of real property. It is the *only* method whereby specific value determinants may be isolated and monetized. Being based on market transactions, it can utilize more facts, and requires fewer estimates, than any other valuation approach.

Once a few basic regressions have been run, the time saving in the appraisal process will be considerable. For instance, after a regression analysis has been run for a particular residential neighborhood or for a particular type of commercial property, the next appraisal in that neighborhood or of that property type may be done by merely applying the equation to the property data in a matter of seconds. A new equation may be run every few months, or whenever a measurable change in the market has occurred.

Additional refinements would never perfect the orthodox sale adjustment process. No standard, widely applicable factor can be derived for second bath, for basement, for 2-car carport vs. 1-car carport, etc., as every neighborhood has its own peculiar weighting of value factors at a given time. The only objective method by which these value determinants may be extracted is by multiple regression analysis.

Another benefit of the process is that it forces the appraiser to reason more rigorously, as each factor must be turned into a number before it can be used. For example, the *judgment* "better location" must be converted to the *fact* "two blocks closer to 100% intersection."

It is easily apparent that this process will require some re-thinking in regard to some of our traditional practices. For example, when a homeowner wants a rough guide for an offering price, and if the appraiser can sit at his desk 300 miles from the property and, given only a few major descriptive items about the property, can price it within

5% of the actual sale price, and do so in a few seconds, would it really be more professional of him to go and inspect the property and go through the lengthy procedure of a traditional appraisal which, when completed, will be no more accurate? Or would he really be wasting his and his client's time performing an irrelevant and obsolete ritual?

The technique of multiple regression analysis still has several shortcomings. One problem is the distortion of individual coefficients by multicollinearity, the effect of relationships between independent variables as well as their relationship with the dependent variable.

Occasional, extreme individual predicting errors also are a defect. While the average error can often be held lower than that obtained by orthodox appraisal methods, the *range* of error is often undesirably high. (For example, the appraiser would most likely prefer a series of errors of +5%, -5%, +5%, -5%, -5% and +5% to a series of 0, -2%, +3%, -5%, and +15%, although the average error is the same.)

These are not fatal defects, however, and it may be anticipated that the technique will be improved with its growing use. At the present state of development, it is not advisable to accept blindly all regression analysis results without a final test by old-fashioned common sense.

Regression analysis is a powerful tool; use of the computer makes it practicable for all sorts of valuation problems in which substantial quantities of data are available. In an active market, it should be a major valuation approach.

XVII

Highest and Best Use Analysis

T he highest and best use analysis is a study of alternative uses for a given site, resulting in a determination of the most profitable, probable legal use of that site.

The highest income does not necessarily represent the highest and best development of the property, for two reasons:

(1) The use may involve depletion of the property.

(2) The income may entail a high risk factor, resulting in lower value. The residual land value, then, is a product of three factors: (1) Obtainable income, (2) Rate of return, and (3) Cost of improvements.

In some cases, an interim use may be indicated, as a more profitable use may be feasible, but at a deferred date. In this case, the deferred use value should be discounted to the present date.

The site may have more than one "best" use; that is, two alternative uses may result in approximately the same land value. On the other hand, it is not proper to assign one use for land and a different use for improvements, at the same time. The most common instances of this fallacy include (1) assignment of land value derived from sales of office building sites, combined with a value assigned to residential or other low

183

intensity improvements, which would have to be removed for construction of an office building; and (2) assignment of land value "as if vacant" for commercial use, plus assignment of value to existing industrial improvements. In such cases, the appraiser should make one of two choices:

(1) If the site is ready for development for a different use, the land value should be assigned for that use, and no improvement value assigned, as the improvements would be razed.

(2) If a deferred higher use is anticipated. an interim use may be assigned, a date estimated for the re-development, and value of the higher use discounted to present worth.

There are two distinct uses of the term "highest and best use," which the appraiser should distinguish:

(1) Use from a social viewpoint, or highest and best use for the community as a whole. This is the planner's problem, not the appraiser's.

(2) Use from an economic point of view, or highest and best use for the specific owner. This is the appraiser's problem.

Two important factors in any highest and best use study have been pointed out by John Rowlson[1]:

(1) The contemplated use must compete with other logical, legal, and economically sound uses.

(2) The analysis entails a very careful study of the legal description of the property, since it is the use of various property rights which is under analysis.

A probable use which is often ignored, but which is very much a part of the market, is what has been designated by Max Derbes[2] as speculative use, which is a purchase and holding of a property strictly for profitable re-sale purposes, rather than for improvement of the site. In this regard, it is interesting to note that ther very case from which the most used definition of market value is derived (Heilbron vs. Sacramento Railroad Company), in 1906, permitted testimony of one of the appraisers as to value of the property for the sole purpose of holding for later re-sale. When no foreseeable improved use is evident, and the property is a part of the speculative use market, then this sector of the market sets the most probable use for the property.

The steps in the highest and best use study are as follows:

(1) Analyze the neighborhood, surrounding uses, trend of development, present use of subject.

(2) Site analysis: topography, size and shape, present use, zoning, possibility of zoning change, and compatibility with surrounding uses.

(3) Analyze the market for each likely use. The uses which are not probable should be eliminated as early in the analysis as possible. Determine the uses available under zoning and deed restrictions; establish the compatibility of the proposed use with

---

[1] John Rowlson, "Highest and Best Use," *The Real Estate Appraiser*, April 1966.

[2] Max Derbes, "Speculative Use Value," *The Appraisal Journal*, April, 1964.

surrounding uses. Account for ancillary needs such as parking, loading area and trackage. Principal property types to be analyzed are:

      (A) Residential

      (B) Apartment

      (C) Hotel, motel

      (D) Retail

      (E) Office building

      (F) Parking

      (G) Industrial

      (H) Interim use

(4) Establish the project scale. Obviously, a successful thirty story building is more likely to produce a higher land value than a one story building. The problem, therefore, is not necessarily in every case to maximize, but to optimize the investment return. The limitations of the particular client's likely project scale is an important factor.

(5) Cost of improvements. In estimating the cost of proposed improvements, two items often overlooked are the time discount and the project carrying costs.

(6) Establish the absorption rate, and staging of the project, discounting for time involved. An approximate land allocation must be made in cases where more than one land use is projected.

(7) Income and expense schedules for each use analyzed.

(8) Assign a rate of return for each use. Since this type of study is normally made for the client who is to use the land, it is practicable and desirable to analyze the return on the basis of net after-tax equity yield.

(9) The tentatively proposed use reflecting the greatest residual value to land is selected as the highest and best use for the site.

XVIII

Feasibility Studies

The purpose of a feasibility study is to estimate the rate of return obtainable for a specific project, on a given site, and to determine whether the proposed project is economically sound *or not*. The "or not," while ungrammatical, is believed essential, as it appears to have been eliminated from consideration in a substantial proportion of feasibility studies the author has read.

The rate of return established is not necessarily a market-level return, but is the possible return for the specific project. This type of study, again, is normally for a specific investor and should be made on the basis of an after-tax net equity yield. Pre-opening costs and discount for time delay in completion of the project must be allowed for.

Generalized Steps:

The steps in a feasibility study may be generalized as follows:

(1) Analysis of supply and of competition.

(2) Analysis of demand; population, income, ability to pay rents or to buy products or utilize services.

(3) Establish rate of absorption.

(4) Sales or rental potentials.

(5) Establish project costs.

(6) Analyze operating expenses, debt service, and depreciation allowance; establish the rate of net return.

(7) Establish equity and mortgage ratios, cash flow, default ratio, and net after-tax equity yield.

Specific Steps:

Following are examples of four specific applications:

I. Office Building (from R. L. Klaasen, *Appraisal Institute Magazine,* Appraisal Institute of Canada, December, 1965): The owner of a vacant site was interested in construction of an office building to be occupied primarily by medical doctors, dentists, and architects. The appraiser's procedure was as follows:

1. Lists were compiled of doctors, dentists and architects practicing in the city during the past ten years.

2. Per capita numbers were analyzed, and projected in accordance with predicted population increases.

3. Note was made of all who had moved into new office space during the past three years.

4. The required number of tenants was calculated by checking the typical sizes of office areas in existing comparable buildings.

5. Existing and proposed competitive space was inventoried.

6. On the basis of the foregoing, the percentage of the proposed building which would be readily absorbed was estimated, and an absorption period estimated for the balance of the building area.

II. Residential Subdivision:

1. Determine number of lots feasible.

2. Estimate retail prices of the lots.

3. Establish, by comparison, the probable rate of absorption of the lots.

4. Obtain cost of on-site and off-site improvements and engineering expenses.

5. Establish overhead and administrative expenses.

6. Establish selling expenses.

7. Assign a rate of profit to the developer.

8. Discount the lot sales either by using present worth of one per annum times average sales, or, preferably, present worth of one deferred for each year's sales. The discount sales, less cost of improvements, administrative and selling expenses, and profit, results in the warranted investment in the raw land. Conversely, if raw land cost is known, the rate of profit is derived.

III. Industrial. (This procedure, generalized for application to any industry, is adapted from: "Feasibility Study of a Proposed Structural Clay Products Industry in

Re-development Area A, Northwest Florida," by George Aase and Associates, Inc. for U.S. Department of Commerce.)

    1. Market analysis

        A. Types and uses of the product.

        B. Production and consumption.

        C. Regional production and marketing characteristics.

        D. Marketing potential for subject.

            (1) Selection and evaluation of plant site.

            (2) Identifying market area.

            (3) Extent and characteristics of market areas.

            (4) Consumption and demand.

            (5) Conclusion as to marketable commodities.

            (6) Prospects for capturing market.

            (7) Transportation analysis.

            (8) Estimate of probable market share.

            (9) Possibilities for expanding present market.

         (10) Conclusions as to sufficiency of market and prospects for future growth.

    2. Raw materials.

        A. Location.

            (1) Subject area.

            (2) Sampling and testing areas.

        B. Feasibility of raw materials production.

            (1) Reserves.

            (2) Quality.

            (3) Extraction methods.

            (4) Transportation.

    3. Plant design and cost estimates.

        A. Capacity and operating schedule.

        B. Process description.

        C. Manpower requirements and labor costs.

        D. Installation costs.

        E. Analysis of costs and returns.

        F. Required conditions for profitable plant operation.

    4. Additional factors affecting feasibility.

        A. Availability and cost of sites.

        B. Labor.

        C. Utilities.

        D. Taxes.

        E. Criteria for plant site selection.

        F. Conclusions.

IV. Motel:

  Following are the steps taken in analyzing the feasibility of a proposed motel:

1. Existing supply was analyzed:

A. Accommodations listed in the AAA Tour Guide with "Good" or better rating were considered competitive.

B. Ratios were established for subject city and several comparable cities for:

(1) Number of rooms to population.

(2) Number of rooms to number of business establishments.

C. Building permit records were studied, to establish average number of rooms constructed per year.

2. Demand was analyzed: comparison of the foregoing ratios indicated a market for the proposed units.

3. Rental rates were estimated, by comparison of the proposed accommodations with the competitive units.

4. Project cost was estimated.

5. Cash flows were projected, and rate of return derived. At this point, the study picks up at the point illustrated in the cash flow projection shown in Chapter XI. In this case, the after-tax return is projected at 11-3/8% to a maximum of 13.5%, with optimum holding period between 8 and 11 years. Since the return is acceptable to the investor, the project is considered feasible.

XIX

Analysis of Proposed
Modernization, Remodeling,
Expansion Programs: Payback
Method; Discounted
Cash Flow Method

The appraiser and consultant occasionally find it necessary to analyze the economic feasibility of a proposed program of modernization, remodeling, or expansion. There are two basic approaches to this problem:

(1) The payback method, and
(2) The discounted cash flow method.

Payback Method:

The payback method is simply the determination of the period of time over which the investment is recoupled. For example, supposing a net investment of $50,000, and a net cash flow of $10,000 per year, then the payback period is five years. Note, however, that this is not a 20% return, but is merely a return *of* the investment in five years. There may, in fact, be no return *on* the investment at all.

The advantages of the payback method are that it is easily calculated and that it gives an easy measure by which alternative investments may be compared. Its disadvantages are that it does not account for the economic life of the project, does not reflect returns received after the end of the payback period, and assigns primary consideration to the recovery period, which may or may not actually be of prime importance.

Discounted Cash Flow Method:

This method of analyzing the investment separately discounts the net cash flow for each year of the life of the proposed project, using the familiar present worth of one factor for discounting. This method takes cognizance of the fact that the pattern of returns is crucial, and that returns which average the same are not necessarily of the same present value. In applying a discounted cash flow analysis, there are two alternative situations with respect to the rate of return:

1. The rate of return may be given. In this case, the minimum acceptable return rate is stated, and the appraiser estimates the present worth of the series of cash flows at this given rate. This minimum, or cut-off rate should be at least in the amount of the cost of capital to the investor, or in the case of a large plant or firm, the return on total plant or firm investment. This rate may quite possibly be different from the return on a comparable real estate investment.

2. Determination of the rate of return may be the objective of the analysis. In this case, trial Present Worth of One rates are used, then bracketed.

Since this type of analysis is for a specific client under specific conditions, the return should be calculated on an after tax basis or the resulting analysis would be useless to the particular client.

It should be noted that, in comparison with the discounted cash flow analysis, an "average rate of return" overstates the return over a period of time, while the return calculated on the original investment understates the return. Discounted cash flow, on the other hand, separately discounts each year's income. In this respect, it is a similar calculation to that for stock and bond yields, and an investor may easily compare the return with returns from other classes of investments.

In estimating the amount of the investment, the amount of outlay should be accounted for exactly, regardless of book figures, for which a number of items may possibly have been expensed, but which for investment purposes are part of the net investment.

Profitability Index:

The profitability index is a measure for the present value of cash flows as compared with the total net investment. When the sum of the present values of the cash flows equals the original investment, then the profitability index equals one. If the index is less than one, the project is not acceptable.

$$\text{Profitability index} = \frac{\text{Net worth of cash flows}}{\text{Investment}}$$

Net Investment:

This does not always necessarily include only the cash paid out: when an asset is used in the project which would otherwise have been sold, the realizable price is a part of the project cost. Also, when an asset would otherwise be used in plant operations or in the business, but is assigned to a proposed project, then its value is a part of the net investment for that project. The cash from disposal of an old asset preparatory to installation of a new asset, when adjusted for tax differences, reduces the net investment.

Residual Value:

In addition to the annual cash flows, there may be a residual value to the asset at the end of project life. The cash realized from disposal of the asset at the end of the project life, adjusted for taxes, is added to the cash flows and discounted to present value.

Example of Discounted Cash Flow Analysis:

The following project is analyzed as an example of application of a discounted cash flow technique: The client is interested in installing central air conditioning in a building which presently has window units. The central system will cost $100,000; installation will require approximately six months. Salvage value of the existing window units is $5,000. The net investment can be reduced by obtaining a mortgage of $50,000 for ten years, at 8% interest rate. The equipment is estimated to have an economic life for tax purposes of fifteen years, with salvage value of $5,000. Double declining balance depreciation will be taken, switching to straight line when this becomes favorable. Tax rate is 50%. Acceptable return is 9%. This proposed project would be analyzed as shown in Figures 19.1 and 19.2.

DISCOUNTED CASH FLOW ANALYSIS

Net Investment:

New Investment	$100,000	
6 Mo.'s Completion Time	4,500	$104,500
100,000 - ½ Yr. @ 9%		
Salvage, Window Units	5,000	
(Depreciated Out) Capital		
Gains Tax	1,250	3,750
		100,750
Loan Obtainable, 10 Yrs. @ 8%		50,000
Net Investment............$		50,750

Figure 19.1

	1	2	3	4	5	6	7	8	9	10	11	12
Yr.	Increased Income	Increased Expense	Net	Interest	Amort.	Depre-ciation	3-(4+6) Taxable Net	.5x7 Tax or (Tax Saving)	3-(4+5) Cash Flow Before Tax	9-8 Cash Flow After Tax	P.W. Factor	P.W.
1	$16,500	$1,000	$15,500	$3,877	$3,407	$12,666	$(1,043)	$(522)	$ 8,216	$8,738	.917431	$ 8,017
2				3,594	3,690	10,978	928	464		7,288	.841680	6,134
3				3,287	3,997	9,514	2,699	1,350		6,866	.772183	5,302
4				2,956	4,328	8,245	4,299	2,150		6,066	.708425	4,297
5				2,597	4,687	7,146	5,757	2,878		5,338	.649931	3,469
6		1,500	15,000	2,208	5,076	6,193	6,599	3,300	7,716	4,416	.596267	2,633
7				1,786	5,498	5,367	7,847	3,924		3,792	.547034	2,074
8				1,330	5,954	4,652	9,018	4,509		3,207	.501866	1,609
9				836	6,448	4,320	9,844	4,922		2,794	.460428	1,286
10				301	6,915	4,320	10,379	5,190		2,526	.422411	1,067
11						4,320	10,680	5,340	15,000	9,660	.387533	3,744
12						4,320	10,680	5,340		9,660	.355535	3,434
13						4,320	10,680	5,340		9,660	.326179	3,151
14						4,320	10,680	5,340		9,660	.299246	2,891
15						4,319	10,681	5,340		9,660	.274538	2,652
												$51,760
15	Salvage value									5,000	.274538	1,373
												$53,133

Profitablity Index = 1.05

DISCOUNTED CASH FLOW ANALYSIS
Figure 19.2

Comparison with Payback Method Results:

The results from the preceding cash flow analysis may be compared with results from the payback method applied to the same figures: Based on the first year after tax income of $8,738, net investment of $50,750 divided by $8,738 equals 5.81 year payback period; based on the net income before depreciation, results are: $50,750 divided by $15,500 equals 3.27 years; based on cash flow before tax, results are: $50,750 divided by $8,216 equals 6.18. Actually, all of these computations are incorrect, as the value of the individual annual cash flows may be determined only by adding the cash flow after tax (column 10). By this method, it may be seen that the correct payback period would be ten years. The payback method, therefore, does not properly account for time discount applicable to the individual series of annual cash flows.

In the example, the minimum return rate was given. In this case, the profitability index was calculated by dividing present worth of total cash flows by the net investment, giving a profitability index of 1.05.

In some cases the return rate would not be given, and the problem would be to determine the rate of return obtained on the project. To apply this approach to the same example, the problem is set up in exactly the same manner through Column 10. The Net Investment, $50,750, is known. This figure is used as the target, and present worth factors for a guessed rate are applied. If the resulting total is below the target figure, the rate is lowered; if above the target, the rate is increased. This trial and error process is not as lengthy as may be imagined, for it is very seldom that more than three trial rates will be needed.

As Basic Valuation Process:

It may be easily seen that the discounted cash flow process has wider application than the valuation of proposed expansion, modernization, etc., and may be used as a basic valuation process for income properties. It is considerably more accurate than the traditional income valuation process, as it properly accounts for such fluctuating income levels over the income projection period as are ascertainable. As was demonstrated in Chapter XII, averaging fluctuating incomes does not reflect the correct valuation, as does separate discounting of each year's income.

The present availability of inexpensive desktop computers and of larger "on line" facilities makes this this sort of analysis and that shown in Chapter XI practicable for even the one-man appraisal office.

XX

Consultation Problems

While consultation problems vary widely, each is handled in basically the same manner:

1. Define the problem. Properly stating the real question often indicates the most likely solution. The problem is not always necessarily what the client thinks it is.

2. Classify the type of problem: feasibility of total project, or of modernization or renovation, highest and best use of the land, rent survey, buy-lease problem, sell-hold problem, management survey, etc.

3. What are the costs and returns—monetary and non-monetary benefits—expectable from the possible alternative courses of action?

4. What are specific criteria for the client? His needs and financing situation, income tax bracket, areas of expertise, etc.

5. When another expert is needed, such as an architect, accountant, engineer, or attorney, don't hesitate to obtain his services, rather than attempt an amateur substitue job for him.

6. Work the alternative solutions to tentative conclusions only, dropping one as soon as a lesser degree of desirability is evident, so that you may concentrate on the most likely course of action.

203

7. Don't forget that negative advice is often more valuable to the client than approval of his proposed project.

Application of this general approach may be indicated by briefly summarizing a few typical problems:

1. The client is a widow, with $110,000 recently received from a condemnation award, which she needs to re-invest. You must fit the selected investment to her specific needs. She is in a 35% tax bracket, wants the property for long term holding and steady cash return; she is, therefore, not interested in equity increment or double declining depreciation.

The broker selects a number of possible investments, and you analyze the income and financial structure of each, eliminating most from consideration. Some properties with good yields from equity increment are discarded, as are some with good leverage but small cash flow. You select a middle aged, stable apartment with substantial equity investment and steady anticipated cash flow, in a neighborhood with probable long-term desirability.

2. The client has a good commercial site, on a main artery, across from a planned motel, and just off a proposed interchange. It is presently improved with an old wholesale store building. He has an offer, and wants to know whether to accept it, or hold.

You compare the site with similar locations *after* completion of surrounding development, and completion of interchange, then discount this value from the expected completion date to the present. To this is added the present worth of the interim income. This value is compared with the price presently obtainable, and you decide that the property will enhance sufficiently that the client should hold it until the motel and interchange are completed.

3. An older commercial hotel of 300 rooms is for sale at $550,000, and the client is interested in the possibility of buying at the apparently low price, and converting to apartments, and wants your opinion of the feasibility.

You obtain an estimated cost for the conversion, ascertain what type of financing would be available, and make a study of the available market for the proposed apartments, and the likely rentals obtainable. A discounted cash flow analysis is then made on the investment, which shows a Profitability Index of less than one.

An acceptable rate of return is not obtainable on the combined sale price and cost of conversion. One reason is that a substantial portion of present price of the property reflects the value of the land for commercial use, while apartment use would be of much lower intensity. Also, satisfactory financing is not obtainable to justify the cash investment required. You conclude that, at a $350,000 price, the purchase may be justifiable, but is definitely ruled out at the asking price of $550,000.

4. The clients are two brothers, who jointly own a property which they want to divide fairly. The property consists of acreage, part of which is potential subdivision land, and two houses, one more expensive than the other. No exact valuation needs to be placed on the property; they just want to divide it evenly.

You draw a plot plan, and begin shifting possible dividing lines. The cheaper house is to the rear, but a road can be extended along one side to it, and create several useable residential lots. You divide the property to leave one with the better house at the front, but less land, and the other with the cheaper house and the potential lots, and their attorney draws up deeds accordingly.

5. A doctor is re-negotiating a combination lease and franchise for laboratory space in two hospitals. He wants to know the fair rental, and how much he is paying in the form of a franchise.

You make a study of rentals for medical space in the two locations, and arrive by comparison at fair rent for the subject spaces. Then you analyze the hospital accounts. (The appraiser who has not had accounting training would, of course, obtain the services of an accountant for this part of the work.) You find that hospital expenses are prorated to the laboratory spaces, including charges for depreciation of building and fixtures, publicity, research, and administrative expenses.

You separate the expenses which properly could be charged to the department as rental, such as utilities, janitor, etc., so that on completion, you have separate figures for the amount of fair rental, and the amounts actually charged to the department which constitute a franchise payment. With this, the doctor has a basis for negotiating a new lease in which the amount of rental is known and therefore the franchise can be intelligently negotiated.

6. A 50 space trailer park is for sale, and the investor client wants to know if he should buy, in view of the attractive price.

You check the park against the FHA and Mobile Home Manufacturers Association criteria point by point, and find that it is below current standards, most importantly with respect to lot sizes. The operating statement is analyzed. At first glance, it shows a nice profit, but the owner and his wife are the operators, and no salary charge is made, nor is a charge made for the rental value of the house which they occupy on the property.

You investigate the operation of several other trailer parks in the city, and find that the expense of management is the largest expense item. Most important, you find that this item is almost the same for a 50 space park as for a 75 space park. The resulting differential between income and expense indicates that a park with less than 75 spaces is barely feasible at all, and definitely not feasible at the asking price and with hired operators. You therefore advise against the investment.

7. The property is an old school building and site, abandoned for school use; the problem is what to do with it. You make preliminary investigation of its indicated income and value for warehousing space, also its value as industrial land, with the building demolished. The *trend* in industrial land values is also carefully considered.

You find that a reasonable income is presently obtainable for storage use of the building, with the owner paying no taxes, and that land values in the neighborhood are increasing at such a rate that, discounting the likely future value of the land, against the presently obtainable price, it is most profitable to hold and rent out the building for two or three years, with enhancing close-in industrial land prices assuring the safety of the future value.

8. A client is interested in the FHA auctions of large apartment projects, and wants suggested bid prices which will be low enough to be profitable, but high enough to have a chance of acquiring the property.

You make a study of the 50 most recent project sales, analyzing each down to estimated net income and equity return. A multiple regression analysis is run on the 50 sales, using as independent variables the number of rooms, the age, whether high or low rise, gross income, net income, and equity income. An estimating equation is obtained which appears to be a fairly reliable predictor of sale price. This figure is used in preliminary selection of projects for bidding, and as one bid indicator, the other being a specific analysis of the equity return for the property being bid on.

Real estate counseling is the most challenging professional function of the appraiser. At this point, he is not simply furnishing a "single figure" value estimate with no regard for its use, as he does in his function as an appraiser, but enters actively into the decision-making process.

Even the beginning appraiser should keep this goal in mind. Although his function is confined principally to the appraisal process during this earlier period, he can be accumulating data files and an extensive library and tackling the more difficult appraisal assignments which will prepare him for the counseling process. I do not subscribe to the dictum that the young appraiser should never accept an assignment of a type which he has never done before. When I read this "rule," I wonder how the author of the rule adhered to it, when performing his first assignment.

The appraiser should at all times be working toward the point at which, as counselor or consultant, he becomes a functional and vital member of the decision-making team. It is only then that the real estate analyst is put to his highest and best use.

INDEX